2nd Edition

Needs
Assessment
BASICS

Beth McGoldrick and Deborah Tobey

atd
PRESS

ATD Press is an internationally renowned source of insightful and practical information on talent development, workplace learning, and professional development.

ATD Press
1640 King Street
Alexandria, VA 22314 USA

Ordering information: Books published by ATD Press can be purchased by visiting ATD's website at www.td.org/books or by calling 800.628.2783 or 703.683.8100.

Library of Congress Control Number: 2016948058

ISBN-10: 1-56286-774-1
ISBN-13: 978-1-56286-774-4
e-ISBN: 978-1-56286-569-6

ATD Press Editorial Staff
Director: Kristine Luecker
Manager: Christian Green
Community of Practice Manager, Learning & Development: Amanda Smith
Senior Associate Editor: Melissa Jones
Cover Design: Anthony Julian
Text Design: Iris Sanchez
Printed by Versa Press, Inc., East Peoria, IL

Contents

About the Training Basics Series

ATD's Training Basics series recognizes and, in some ways, celebrates the fast-paced, ever-changing reality of organizations today. Jobs, roles, and expectations change quickly. One day you might be a network administrator or a process line manager, and the next day you might be asked to train 50 employees in basic computer skills or to instruct line workers in quality processes.

Where do you turn for help? The ATD Training Basics series is designed to be your one-stop solution. The series takes a minimalist approach to your learning curve dilemma and presents only the information you need to be successful. Each book in the series guides you through key aspects of training: giving presentations, making the transition to the role of trainer, designing and delivering training, and evaluating training. The books in the series also include some advanced skills, such as performance and basic business proficiencies.

The ATD Training Basics series is the perfect tool for training and performance professionals looking for easy-to-understand materials that will prepare nontrainers to take on a training role. In addition, this series is the consummate reference tool for any trainer's bookshelf and a quick way to hone your existing skills.

Preface

It has been more than 10 years since the first edition of this book was written. In that time, the world has changed substantially. With the financial crisis starting in 2008 that continues to challenge organizations today, as well as outbreaks of war and terrorism, many organizations are hesitant to make additional investments in hiring more people, and thus are expecting more out of the people on their payrolls. Organizations need their current employees to be more efficient and more effective. This is where training and other HRD professionals can make a huge impact.

Over the past few years, training professionals have built inroads into helping organizations design, develop, and implement training programs that help organizations overcome knowledge and skill problems, successfully introduce new products into the marketplace, and help them succeed in doing more with less. However, there is still room to build a stronger relationship between training professionals and the organizations they work with through performance consulting.

What's New in This Edition?

In this second edition, you'll see:

- a greater emphasis on how a training professional can move from being a training order taker to being a valued performance consultant
- information on implementing a return on expectations (ROE) focus in which the client has expectations for the results of the training program, but doesn't want to pursue a return on investment (ROI) strategy
- a stronger link for human performance improvement (HPI) to help organizations with the systematic and systemic discovery of the root causes that prevent them from getting the results they desire.

Who Should Read This Book?

This book is still designed for new or established training professionals—instructional designers, trainers, or training department managers—who want to make sure that their training programs meet the performance needs of their organizations. If you're reading this book, it's likely that your goals are to develop the foundation that will ensure the training programs you design and deliver will help the organization succeed.

How This Book Is Organized

To successfully assess training needs, you need to be able to identify the context for a training course request at four separate stages. You'll also have to identify the big picture of training needs throughout the organization. This book can help you do that. Here's a summary of the 10 chapters in *Needs Assessment Basics:*

Chapter 1, "Why Needs Assessment?" gives you an overview of the book. It focuses on the multiple purposes of needs assessment and serves as a foundational layer for the rest of the book.

Chapter 2, "The Training Request," shows you how to begin analyzing training needs within the most common framework encountered by trainers: receiving a training request from a client or manager in your organization. You will learn about the four stages of data collection required for thorough needs assessment and about the challenge of creating internal credibility so that you can conduct your needs assessment.

Chapter 3, "Identifying Questions and Data Sources," helps you identify questions that must be answered by the training needs assessment. You will also discover how to identify the sources that will provide the necessary data with the help of your business partners and client.

Chapter 4, "Evaluating Potential Data Collection Methods," offers guidance on how to choose data collection methods to answer the identified questions using the selected data sources. When comparing data collection methods, you must consider time and resource constraints, and realize that certain methods work best for certain information needs.

Chapter 5, "Data Collection Implementation," offers guidance in the ultimate choice of data collection methods and provides some tips and techniques for carrying out the data collection process.

Chapter 6, "Data Analysis," discusses what you discover—what the data tell you about the training need being investigated. One of the most important points is the fact that data are not the same things as recommendations.

Chapter 7, "Data Analysis Recommendations," demonstrates the difference between data and recommendations. Recommendations are the needs assessor's actual conclusions and suggested actions that she thinks should be carried out. The needs assessor's role in identifying issues that are unrelated to training is also examined.

Chapter 8, "Communicating With Your Client," presents communication techniques that can assist you in reaching your goal: the implementation of your recommendations to help the business improve. You will explore planning a presentation tailored to a specific client and stakeholders.

Chapter 9, "The Ideal Organization Scan," goes beyond the real-world training needs assessment approach presented in this book. In the real world you often find yourself reacting to training requests. In a perfect world, you would have the time and resources to be proactive and engage your client by continuously scanning the organization and the external environment for information indicating trends and patterns in organization needs and training implications. Call it the investigative reporter approach, named after the many television and newspaper reporters who are always taking in and processing information to uncover problems in their city, their country, and the world.

Chapter 10, "A Final Note," offers some food for thought about the role of training needs assessment in the organization, what to do when you don't have time to conduct a proper needs assessment, the field of performance consulting, and ideas for further professional development.

The book also includes references and additional resources, which provide many sources to support your professional growth.

Each chapter opens with a quick access guide—What's Inside This Chapter—to introduce you to the contents of the chapter. Use this section to identify the information it contains and, if you wish, skip ahead to the material most useful to you.

The final section of each chapter—Getting It Done—supports your ability to take the content of that chapter and apply it. A progressive case study will be featured to challenge you in understanding and using the chapter content. You will also find tools that will assist you in applying the concepts to your own situation. Sometimes the tool is a list of questions for you to ponder, sometimes it is a self-assessment questionnaire, and sometimes it is a list of action steps you can take to enhance your training needs assessment skills.

This book strives to make it as easy as possible for you to understand and apply its lessons. Icons throughout the book help you identify key points that can mean the difference between needs assessment success or failure.

Basic Rules

These rules cut to the chase. They are unequivocal and important concepts in the area of training needs assessment.

Noted

This icon is used to give you more detail or explanation about a concept or a principle. It is also occasionally used for a short but productive tangent.

Think About This

These are helpful tips that you can "put in your back pocket" to pull out when needed as you conduct a needs assessment.

Acknowledgments

I dedicate this book to my husband, John McGoldrick, for being a blessing to me and my biggest fan; my parents, Robert and Diane Richards; and my inlaws, Joe and Joanne Zoppa. I also want to thank Steve Villachica, who has been my adviser and my mentor. Thank you to Deborah Tobey for beginning this work and for ATD for giving me the opportunity. Finally I want to thank all of my colleagues, both at work and online, who have encouraged me to continuously improve and to help the organizations I work with do the same.

Beth McGoldrick
September 2016

Preface to the First Edition

This book is for training professionals—instructional designers, trainers, or training department managers—who want to make sure that their training programs meet the performance needs of their organizations. If you're reading this book, it's likely that your goals are to develop the foundation that will ensure the training programs you design and deliver will:

- Have a bottom-line impact on the business needs of your organization.
- Ensure that employee performance on the job contributes to that impact.
- Make certain that the ultimate training design is skill-based to support employee performance back on the job.
- Guarantee that the training delivery and facilitation are attuned to the learning needs of the participants and support an environment of learning.

The purpose of this book is to increase your understanding and experience with conducting training needs assessments and, even more important, to gain your commitment to using needs assessment as the foundation for effective training design, development, delivery, and evaluation.

One caveat: You will notice that the assumption in this book is that the reader is an internal training staff person in an organization. If you are an external trainer or consultant, these methods will work for you as well. Any special considerations for external consultants are highlighted along the way.

I dedicate this book to my husband, Bryan Tobey, and my parents, Barbara and Dale Davis. My sincere thanks go to my friend and colleague Don McCain for his continuing support, listening ear, and suggestions. And, to all of my colleagues over the years whose interaction has stimulated and buoyed me, thanks to you most of all!

Deborah Tobey
April 2005

1

Why Needs Assessment?

 What's Inside This Chapter

This chapter provides an overview of the book, focusing on the multiple purposes of needs assessment and serving as a foundation for the rest of the book.
You'll learn:

- definitions of some important terms
- the purposes of training needs assessment
- the phases in training needs assessment
- how the training needs assessment sets the stage for training evaluation.

1

Why Needs Assessment?

Introduction: An Analogy

In spring 1985, the developers at Coca-Cola Company came out with a new flavor of Coke, removing traditional Coca-Cola from all store shelves, vending machines, restaurants, and bars. From that point on, only "new Coke" was available. Do you remember what happened? The public hated it—they refused to buy new Coke. The huge uproar resulted in Coca-Cola bringing back "old Coke" just 79 days later, now renamed Coca-Cola Classic.

What happened here? Coca-Cola is a large company, well loved by customers not just for its beverages, but for the nostalgia the brand evokes for its customers and its ties to the history of many countries. However, Coke sales and consumer awareness were down in 1985 and the company sought to do something about it. Unfortunately Coca-Cola didn't appear to do a needs assessment to find out the real problems behind falling Coke sales before forging ahead with what it thought customers wanted, rather than what it turned out they appeared to want. The company made a huge mistake that cost it millions of dollars and loyal customers.

If you have good data that help you understand what the real problem is, then you can solve it, save the company money, and satisfy your employees and customers.

What Is Training Needs Assessment?

Simply put, training needs assessment is the process of identifying how training can help your organization reach its goals. "Training needs assessment is what you do to create the tangible solution(s) to the problem or opportunity" (Rossett 2009). It's interesting that the words *training, skills,* and *learning* do not appear in that definition. One important aspect of a needs assessment is that it helps training professionals provide input for the ultimate training design. However, an even more important feature of a needs assessment is establishing that there is a business need, driving a performance need, driving a true training need, identifying the specifics regarding the desired training, and finally, identifying the nontraining issues that are also present and affecting the performance situation. Training can help businesses and organizations solve problems and prepare for opportunities.

Although training itself certainly provides skills and learning and development, the training needs assessment is the preliminary process that ensures the training is grounded in the needs of the organization. Without a needs assessment, trainers risk developing and delivering training programs that do not support organizational needs and, therefore, do not deliver value to the organization or the client. And, the training that is developed may not be accepted by the target audience, or worse, the training may end up being useless and a waste of everyone's time

Implementing a proper training needs assessment helps the organization see the value of the training function and its role as a business partner. Establishing a collaborative relationship with the client during the needs assessment develops a pattern of involvement and joint decision making that can continue throughout the design, delivery, and evaluation steps of the training process. This allows the business stakeholders to be involved in uncovering and solving the true performance problem.

Defining Key Terms

Before beginning an in-depth examination of training needs assessment, two terms that are used throughout this book must be defined: *needs assessor* and *client*.

A needs assessor may be a training, HRD, or HR staff member of an organization who is responsible for the design and delivery of training solutions and is, therefore, responsible for training needs assessment. Alternatively, a needs assessor may be an external training, HRD, or HR professional who works with client organizations to design and deliver training. Anyone reading this book is probably a needs assessor—or will be soon. In this book, the term *needs assessor* is used when referring to individuals in their strict role within the needs assessment process. If a more general or universal comment is necessary, the term *training professional* is used.

The client is the individual that the needs assessor is working with to design and develop the training program. That individual might be a department manager, a department head, or the CEO. Think of the client as the person who will benefit the most from the increased performance of the employees who will participate in the training program. On occasion, an internal professional might have an additional client: his own manager. For example, if you work in HR and the HR director (the boss) is driving the training project or is invested in the outcome in some way, the HR director would also be the client. And, yes, that means you would be working for two clients.

Basic Rule 1

Needs assessment measures set the foundation for evaluation measures. Start with the end in mind.

Purposes of a Training Needs Assessment

A training needs assessment, when implemented effectively, serves multiple purposes:

- It places the training need or request in the context of the organization's needs. Training adds value only when it ultimately serves a business need.
- It validates and augments the initial issues presented by the client. Clients know their business, no doubt about it! But, sometimes they don't know the cause of or remedy for issues that involve human performance. The needs assessment can reveal different information, provide broader context for the information supplied by the client, and offer different perspectives on the client's initial impressions.
- It ensures that the ultimate training design supports employee performance and thereby helps the organization meet its needs. A significant portion of a training needs assessment encompasses gathering information to support the training design, identify and capture skills and knowledge, and ensure that the design replicates the learners' jobs as closely as possible.
- It results in recommendations regarding nontraining issues that are affecting the achievement of the desired organization and employee performance goals. The main question is this: If the ultimate training program is perfect, what else is going on in the organization that will result in the business needs not being met? There are several reasons why it is critical that the needs assessor identify these issues and provide recommendations to rectify them. First, there is a much greater likelihood of achieving the desired business and performance results. Second, the training function is held accountable for only the portion of the business and performance needs that it can influence. Third, it increases the value added by the training function to the organization. (Now can you see why the Coke versus new Coke illustration is an apt analogy?)

- It helps ensure the survival of the training function. When a training program adds value, the training function is valued for its impact and results and is not at high risk during hard times.
- It establishes the foundation for back-end evaluation. Although this book is about front-end needs assessment, rather than back-end measurement and evaluation, the relationship between the two is very clear. In training and other HRD initiatives, you always start with the end in mind. What do you want people to do that they are not doing now, or what do you want them to do differently from what they are doing now. And how will you know it when you see it? Figure 1-1 illustrates how a needs assessment sets the stage for evaluation. During a training needs assessment, measures are taken at four stages (left side of Figure 1-1): business needs, performance needs, learning needs, and learner needs. During evaluation (which occurs after the training program), the evaluator takes measurements of the same items—now called the four levels of evaluation: learner reaction, learning (knowledge and skill mastery), job performance, and business needs. The goal in training is to be able to identify positive changes in each of the four needs assessment pre-measures when they are measured again during evaluation. Note that after the evaluation business measurement is taken, it can result in the start of a new needs assessment.

 Think About This

Training recommendations can also include a return on investment (ROI) or a return on expectations (ROE) forecast. An ROI forecast is a prediction of the comparison between the costs of designing, developing, and delivering the training program and the value of the ultimate expected business outcome the training is expected to influence. Clients use the ROI forecast to help decide if a training project is worthwhile; trainers use it to influence the client's decision. This book deals with ROI briefly as a possible needs assessment outcome or recommendation, and it is covered in much greater detail as an evaluation technique in another volume of this series, *Evaluation Basics*, 2nd edition (McCain 2016). An ROE forecast is a prediction of the client's expectations for behavior change at the end of the training and the value of the expected business outcome that the training is expected to influence. Chapter 10 discusses differences between ROI and ROE.

Figure 1-1. Needs Assessment Sets the Stage for Evaluation

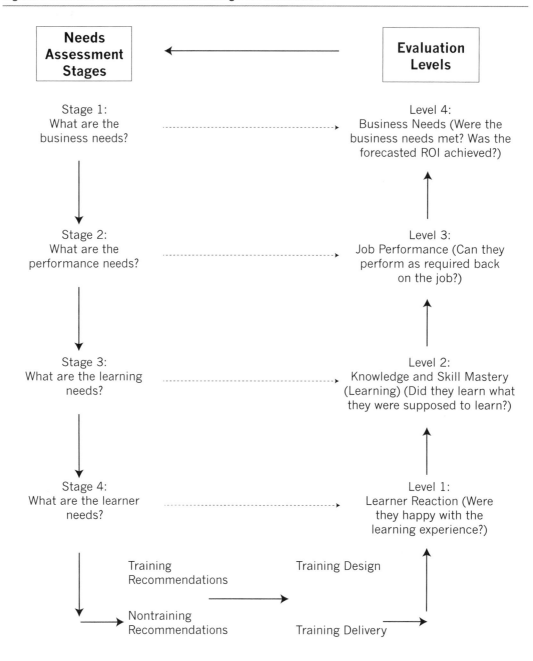

Noted

It's not that evaluation can't be implemented for training initiatives for which no needs assessment was conducted. Back-end evaluation measures can still be taken, and the trainer and client can agree on whether or not the back-end measures meet expectations. A more powerful case for organization and performance improvement (not to mention for training itself) is made by matching the needs identified up front with the measures taken at the end, because it demonstrates impact that can be directly attributed to training. This matchup demonstrates training's added value in a very potent way.

Steps in Training Needs Assessment

The seven steps in training needs assessment are depicted in Figure 1-2, and are described in some detail in the following sections.

Step 1. Conduct an External and Internal Organizational Scan

Training professionals spend a significant amount of time scanning the internal and external environment and gathering information from many sources, such as newspapers, current events, annual reports, financial statements, customer service data, strategic plans, benchmarking, and the break room.

Step 2. Collect Data to Identify Business Needs

From the scanning process, the needs assessor is able to identify the current organizational needs, which fall into three categories:

- an opportunity that must be capitalized upon (for example, a new product or market)
- a problem that must be resolved (for example, waste, customer complaints, poor product quality, absenteeism)
- a business strategy that must be supported (for example, a marketing and product approach that caters to a certain age group, or a hospital that wants to brand itself as "the maternity hospital in the community").

Business needs can be identified at the macro level (the overall organization) or at the micro level (one department or unit, depending on who your client is).

Figure 1-2. The Training Needs Assessment Process

Step 1. Conduct an External and Organization Scan

Step 2. Collect Data to Identify Business Needs

Capitalize on an opportunity
Resolve a problem
Support a strategy

Step 3. Collect Data to Identify Performance, Learning, and Learner Needs

Required performance
Learners' current performance
Required skills and knowledge
Learners' current skills and knowledge
Learner needs

Step 4. Analyze Data

Identify key data: gaps in performance,
skills, and knowledge
Identify recommendations

Step 5. Identify Potential Training Solution

Needed job aids and performance support materials
Types of training methods
Types of training delivery

Step 6. Deliver Data Analysis Feedback

Training recommendations: design and
delivery; ROI or ROE forecast
Nontraining recommendations: work
environment, rewards, consequences,
work processes

Transition Step: Begin Training Design

Step 3. Collect Data to Identify Performance, Learning, and Learner Needs

Multiple sources of data must be addressed to identify desired and current job performance, desired and current skill and knowledge level, and learner needs. Each set of needs will likely include skill deficiencies (training needs) and other issues that affect performance (nontraining needs).

Step 4. Analyze Data

Data analysis yields key information that identifies the gaps between desired and current job performance, and between desired and current knowledge and skill levels, so that the ultimate training design will target those gaps. Understanding the magnitude of these gaps also assists the needs assessor in assigning priorities to the various issues that have to be addressed.

Step 5. Identify Potential Training Solutions

At this point in the process, potential training initiatives have usually been identified by either the needs assessor or the client. Sometimes the needs assessors will approach their clients to share discoveries they made during organizational scanning, and sometimes the clients make the first move.

Step 6. Deliver Data Analysis Feedback

The needs assessor makes a presentation or generates a report for the client detailing data analysis, training recommendations for design and delivery, and nontraining recommendations (recommendations to resolve issues that are not caused by knowledge or skill deficiencies).

Transition Step: Begin Training Design Process

This is where the process segues into design. If the needs assessment has been implemented well, the training designer has ample information to produce targeted learning objectives, learning activities, job-relevant content and materials to support activities, measurement and evaluation tools, and a learning environment.

Each of these steps is explored more fully in later chapters. For now, however, notice that this process includes many steps that occur before a training solution is even mentioned. It is critical that any training initiative undertaken be directly linked to the business needs of the organization through internal and external scanning and identification of business needs before any other work is done. If not, value is not added. This is bad, because if the organization hits a rough spot, functions that haven't added any value are at the highest risk.

 Basic Rule 2

Training needs assessment results in training that supports business needs first and, in so doing, adds value to the organization.

Needs Assessment Basics will provide you with ample food for thought, tools, checklists, and worksheets to help you make these materials and concepts yours. We recommend that you make copies of the checklists and tools, or transfer them to spreadsheets to use as templates for your projects. Ready to get started?

2

The Training Request

 What's Inside This Chapter

This chapter shows you how to begin analyzing training needs within the most common framework encountered by trainers: receiving a training request from a client or manager in your organization. You'll learn:

- that training needs assessment usually begins "near the end," with a training request from a client
- how to handle the initial client conversation about a training request
- what questions to ask a client to identify initial business needs, performance needs, learning needs, and learner needs
- several different ways to handle the training request conversation to increase your credibility.

2

The Training Request

Starting Near the End: The Training Request

You are walking down the hall in your organization minding your own business when you run into a department manager. You greet each other and chat for a moment and then the manager says, "You know, I'm having some trouble with my customer satisfaction measures in the call center. They seem to be in a decline. The phone representatives must not be as responsive to the customers as they should. Would you set up a telephone skills training session next Tuesday?"

Your first instinct would probably be to say, "Yes, certainly! What time?" but why would you agree so readily? Perhaps you believe:

A. You have an excellent telephone skills program that you have been wanting to pilot test, and this would be your chance to do so.

B. The HRD field is a helping profession that resonates for you, and this is an opportunity to help.

C. You are an excellent trainer, and this is a chance to shine.

D. You want to be responsive to your clients and build a reputation of responsiveness. After all, that's your job, isn't it?

E. This manager has a reputation for being demanding and no-nonsense—the only answer this manager is looking for is "yes," and that means a lot of pressure!

So, which option would you choose? Maybe all of the above? These issues exist for training professionals every time they have a conversation like this in the hall or when a manager asks them to stop by to talk about a training need. It's hard *not* to say yes immediately with these pressures.

Now look at the other side of the coin. Why wouldn't saying "Yes, certainly! What time?" be the best response?

A. You don't know how this problem (low customer satisfaction measures) fits into this manager's overall business strategy. (You could end up solving a problem that isn't very important.)

B. You don't know what the customer satisfaction numbers are or what they should be. (There is no business goal to focus on.)

C. You don't know what factors other than the phone representatives' job performance might be contributing to the decline in customer satisfaction measures. (It might not be a training problem at all.)

D. You don't know what the phone representatives are doing wrong. (You might not hit on the skills they need when you deliver your course.)

E. You don't know if the telephone skills course you have matches with what the representatives are doing wrong. (You might train them in skills they already know and miss the skills they need.)

F. You don't know how the phone representatives feel about their job performance or the prospect of participating in telephone skills training. (You could insult them by teaching things they already know and thereby create or contribute to a morale issue.)

G. You don't know what kind of learning environment would be most conducive to the phone representatives' needs as learners. (You could end up delivering a course that's too easy, too challenging, too active, too inactive, too intimidating, or too uncomfortable and thereby impede their learning.)

If you thought that all the reasons listed were valid, you're on the right track. It can be difficult not to give the client an immediate yes, but your short-term gains from being perceived as responsive will be outweighed by the long-term risk of not adding value or having a positive impact on the client's business. Instead, this is when you need to have a training needs conversation with the client; this chapter focuses on that part of the process. In this conversation, you will more than likely say "Yes, and . . . " rather than simply "yes."

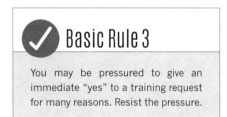

✓ Basic Rule 3

You may be pressured to give an immediate "yes" to a training request for many reasons. Resist the pressure.

Why Start Here?

Remember Figure 1-2, which depicted the training needs assessment process? Figure 2-1 is the same diagram, but with the topic for this chapter highlighted. You'll notice that the highlighted portion is the second step, not the first step, in the process. Why not start at the first step? Why start here?

Figure 2-1. The Training Needs Assessment Process With Step 2 Highlighted

Step 1. Conduct an External and Organization Scan

Step 2. Collect Data to Identify Business Needs

Capitalize on an opportunity
Resolve a problem
Support a strategy

Step 3. Collect Data to Identify Performance, Learning, and Learner Needs

Required performance
Learners' current performance
Required skills and knowledge
Learners' current skills and knowledge
Learner needs

Step 4. Analyze Data

Identify key data: gaps in performance,
skills, and knowledge
Identify recommendations

Step 5. Identify Potential Training Solution

Needed job aids and performance support materials
Types of training methods
Types of training delivery

Step 6. Deliver Data Analysis Feedback

Training recommendations: design and
delivery; ROI or ROE forecast
Nontraining recommendations: work
environment, rewards, consequences,
work processes

Transition Step: Begin Training Design

This book starts at step 2 even though the hallway conversation started at step 5. As you may already know based on your experience, the needs assessor's first challenge is to *step backward* in the process and place the training request in the context of the business needs—step 2. You must guide the conversation in the hallway (or more appropriately, in a scheduled meeting with adequate time allotted) away from identifying a training plan—step 5, where the client started—to a more appropriate focus on the second step in the process: Collect data to identify the business needs.

So, in essence, you have to redirect the conversation to focus on step 2 because your client unknowingly entered the process near the end at step 5. By focusing on step 2, you can express the training need in the context of the client's business needs.

 Noted

Is there ever a time when the process actually begins at the beginning? Yes, it can. In fact, it is a worthy goal for training professionals to continuously scan the organization's internal and external business needs (steps 1 and 2) to identify potential training needs. In a perfect world, all training needs would be identified and explored in this manner (see chapter 9). For now, however, the focus is on how potential training needs are usually identified in the real world: The client initiates the training request.

The Initial Client Conversation

The initial conversation you conduct with your client provides some indicators regarding the client's needs, setting you on the data collection trail (addressed in chapters 3, 4, and 5). However, before starting down that trail, you must identify the business context. This initial conversation, therefore, has multiple goals:

- Identify the client's perceptions of the need that triggered the client to make the training request.
- Place that need in the context of the business by identifying the client's business needs and how the need is linked to the business needs.
- Identify the client's perception of any employee performance needs inherent in the situation.
- Identify the client's perception of what the intended training initiatives should address.
- Identify the client's perception of the employees' needs as learning participants.
- Set the stage for the possibility that there might be training-related and nontraining-related issues contributing to the client's need.

- Gain permission and support for a needs assessment data collection effort to ensure the training will resolve the business and performance needs.
- Establish a reasonable timeframe for the potential training deliverables.

Each set of information provides direction for your data collection efforts in the needs assessment process. Table 2-1 offers some questions that you can use during a client discussion to start identifying indicators for data collection. The questions are organized according to the needs assessment stages that were outlined in Figure 1-1.

Table 2-1. Questions to Ask During an Initial Client Discussion to Trigger Data Collection

Needs Assessment Stage	Questions
Stage 1: Business Needs	• What current business needs or strategies are being affected or perhaps caused by the assumed problem? • What business problems exist? (Look for such measures as amount of increase or decrease in business indicators, including sales, waste, customer satisfaction, turnover, grievances, productivity, quality, and complaints. If the client doesn't know the actual measures, it is critical to find this information during data collection.) • What is going on in the external environment that is related to this problem (for example, competition, market changes, and government regulations)? • What other data exist (that your business unit already collects) that may provide information regarding this business need (such as sales, productivity, quality, HR information, benchmarking, and so forth)? • What change(s) in these business indicators are you seeking to achieve with this training plan? What measures will tell you that you have been successful? • What business opportunities are inherent in this business need (for example, new markets or new products)? • What business strategy(ies) are you seeking to support with this requested training initiative? • What's happening in your business that shouldn't be happening? • What's not happening in your business that should be happening?
Stage 2: Performance Needs	• What results should employees be achieving? What is their current level of achievement? • What should people be doing differently? • What should they stop, start, or keep doing? • What does perfect performance look like? What does current performance look like? • Is anyone performing those skills correctly now? How many people are doing it correctly versus how many are not? • What is the cost to the business of doing it incorrectly? • Is this problem important enough to the organization to do something about it? • What else might be getting in the way of employees performing as they should, other than lack of skills and knowledge (nontraining issues)? • What will the nature of management support be for job application and practice after training?

Needs Assessment Stage	Questions
Stage 3: Learning Needs	• What knowledge and skills do you think the targeted employees need to learn to perform the way they should? • How important is each knowledge item and skill that you have listed? • How well should the targeted employees be performing the skills by the end of the training? • Is anyone performing those skills now? • How well are they performing? Are they meeting business goals?
Stage 4: Learner Needs	• What are the targeted learners' backgrounds and experience in this subject matter? • What is their job environment like (fast paced, stressful, routine)? • What are the expectations regarding when and how they will attend the training (during work, after hours, paid, unpaid)? • What technology do the learners have access to? • How durable does the course need to be? (Does it need to exist for one-time use, a month, a year, or ongoing?) • What access to course documents do learners need before, during, and after the course? (Does there need to be a reference manual, job aids, performance support, or a knowledge management database?)

 Basic Rule 4

In response to a training request, say "Yes—and I have a few questions so I can best fulfill your request and help meet your goal."

Acting on a Hunch

Should you play out a hunch during this initial conversation? For example, what if a client says that training in a certain skill is needed for a group of employees, but your background and experience tell you that the desired training won't resolve the problem at hand? You immediately form an intuitive guess—a hunch—that other resolutions will be more effective than the solution the client has chosen. Hunches are good things; they occur because you have seen patterns, trends, and common cause-and-effect relationships during your experience in needs assessment and training. Many times—if not most of the time—your hunches are correct.

So, should you act on a hunch during this conversation? Should you present other possibilities or begin a line of questioning that dissuades the client from her idea that a specific training solution is the answer? No, not yet. Although the client doesn't have any data at this point to prove her argument, neither do you. Postulating or speculating about solutions that differ from the client's expectations at this time only causes tension. Instead, negotiate to gather data to determine the real cause, which might prove your hunch correct. When the time comes, the data will convince the client.

There are a few other questions you may wish to ask during your initial conversation with the client. You could ask about the possibility of conducting a training needs assessment to collect more information regarding this training initiative. This is also a good opportunity to request access to data sources, such as organizational data collected in the client's department and other departments (for example, customer service or the HR and quality improvement departments), managers of the targeted employees, the targeted employees themselves, aggregate performance appraisal data and trends on the targeted employees, exemplary employees, and subject matter experts.

Dealing With Nontraining Issues

One question listed in Table 2-1 deals with nontraining issues, which comprise such areas as lack of tools, equipment, and resources; lack of policies or procedures to support the desired performance; ineffective or inefficient work processes; lack of management support for skill transfer back on the job after training; lack of incentives and rewards for producing the desired performance; lack of negative consequences for undesirable performance; and lack of clear performance expectations, including feedback on job performance. Some clients may not understand what you mean by nontraining issues that might be getting in the way of performance or they may be reluctant to answer. Others may think you are accusing them of mistakenly choosing training as the solution for a problem. Others might not want to consider nontraining issues because if a training issue has been identified, they have effectively transferred that problem to the training professional. Suggesting that other causes might need to be addressed implies that the client—not the trainer—has to deal with at least part of the problem. Once clients put something on your plate, they usually do not want any part of it handed back.

Building Credibility

Will every client respond positively and collaboratively to the questioning suggested here? Probably not. Many organizations, and managers, view the training professional as a training provider—someone who simply delivers training as requested by the clients and has a limited role in the organization's performance issues. The first time you try to change this perception with a particular client by having a conversation about the needs underlying the training request, you might be met with surprise, impatience, or annoyance.

Think About This

Understanding and identifying performance issues involves a complex thought process. Robert Mager (1997a) developed a performance analysis thought process flowchart that is invaluable in helping sort out training and nontraining issues.

There will be clients who are willing to consider all aspects of what is causing the performance issue. When you ask for permission for your needs assessment, they will gladly give it to uncover the real cause of the problem. With this client, you simply enhance your value as a business partner and consultant by conducting a thorough and effective training needs assessment.

There will be other times when clients force you to prove that your approach works—they will not be giving you the benefit of the doubt! You will simply have to say yes to a perceived training need and then find ways to build aspects of the needs assessment into the delivery of the training. At the end of the project, when you give your clients your evaluation report tell them that you were able to tailor the training to meet their business needs because you built in some needs assessment work as you were developing the training materials. They may be intrigued and ask for more information on how you were able to get your information. You can then share some of the tactics you used to find out what was affecting the desired performance, and show the clients how you weaved that information into the training design to help them meet their business goals. As you begin building credibility with those clients, you'll be able to add needs assessments to future training projects and continue to help them meet their business goals.

Why do it one way with one client and another way with a different client? Client perceptions regarding training professionals vary according to organizational culture, past history with other training professionals, past history with you, perceptions of training that are individual to each client, and understanding of the HRD field. What works with one client will not work with another. If the needs assessor doesn't vary the approach according to the client's characteristics in this initial conversation, opportunities for a positive impact on the business will be lost. The ultimate paradox is that if you don't adjust your approach to focus on building credibility in a way that works in the situation, credibility will never be established.

You are working toward the goal of being a trusted business partner. You may have to start out as a training order taker and then begin building credibility with your clients by including some needs assessment through your instructional design and interviews with subject matter experts. This will move you to the role of training professional. As you build more credibility by providing solutions that help the business improve, you will be afforded more flexibility to include more needs assessment methods in your process. Eventually you will become a performance consultant with business partners relying on your expertise and methods to help them come to the right solutions that solve the business needs.

Do you always have to fulfill a client's training request? How can you maintain your credibility if your hunches, the data, your background, and your experience all indicate that the problem is not a skill deficiency and, therefore, not a training issue? Will you still have to deliver a training solution? The answer is sometimes yes and sometimes no. Sometimes you will be able to follow that old training adage—give them what they need and call it what they want. For example, if they are insistent that their employees need training, you might be able to provide the training they think they need with some of what the data say they need by weaving needs assessment methods into your instructional design process and then include that in the training implementation (more on that in chapter 10).

If you were given permission to conduct a needs assessment, then the client is probably at least somewhat willing to explore other possibilities. Once you have gathered and analyzed your data and the indicators are clear, you should be able to convince these clients, especially if you have good recommendations regarding the nontraining issues you have identified (and if you still deliver some type of training solution as part of the solution).

On the other hand, you will have some clients who are so convinced that training is the only solution that they cannot be persuaded otherwise—at least not until the training plan is delivered and the evidence that it was not a training issue is irrefutable. With these clients, conducting a needs assessment is difficult, if not impossible. Sometimes the best answer is something like: "Yes, I can deliver the telephone skills training next Tuesday, *and* I would also like to use some of the session to gather information about what else might be contributing to the decline in customer satisfaction figures." Then you can deliver both the training program and the value-added needs assessment activities that you propose. This tactic might not secure permission for your needs assessment on the project, but it will build credibility for the next interaction with that client.

So learn how to work with your business partners. Remember that the ultimate goal is to improve the business. When you can work with the client to prove that what you deliver will help the business, then you will gain credibility and become a more valued partner. This will give you more leeway to perform a thorough, effective training needs assessment for future problems and projects.

Getting It Done

How you handle the initial conversation with a potential client about a potential training plan is critical in shaping how you deliver your services to that client and how useful your services will be to the client's business goals. This initial conversation also influences your future relationship with that client and your credibility as a training professional. Exercises 2-1 and 2-2 will help you begin to think about your role as a needs assessor in your organization, and in relation to a specific client you might work with.

As mentioned in the preface, this book features a progressive case study using the chapter content in a situation similar to one you might find in your organization to challenge your understanding. Exercise 2-3 describes a step in the case needs assessment process. You are asked to identify or discuss what Chris, the training professional in the case, should do next. A potential answer is presented in chapter 3 to guide you in evaluating your response.

Exercise 2-1. Importance Assessment

Circle the response below (low, medium, high) that indicates the importance of each training needs assessment purpose as it applies to your organization. Take note of the items that you mark high and jot some notes in the rightmost column to help you prepare to explain those items to your client or manager when called upon to do so.

Purpose of Training Needs Assessment	Importance in My Organization			Explanation
Placing a client's stated training need or request in the context of the organization's needs	Low	Medium	High	
Validating and augmenting the initial issues presented by the client	Low	Medium	High	
Ensuring the ultimate training design supports employee performance and helps the organization meet its needs	Low	Medium	High	
Identifying recommendations regarding nontraining issues that are affecting the achievement of the desired organization and employee performance goals	Low	Medium	High	
Ensuring survival of the training function	Low	Medium	High	
Establishing the foundation for back-end evaluation	Low	Medium	High	

Exercise 2-2. Preparing for the Initial Client Conversation

Think about a client you are working with now. Imagine that this client has asked you into his office and has requested a training program.

Now, consider these questions:

1. What is this client's current perception of what training and HRD professionals do?
2. What is this client's perception of the role of training in supporting business strategies and employee performance?
3. What questions will you ask this client to place the training request in the context of business and performance needs and build credibility to conduct a training needs assessment?

Exercise 2-3. The Whitewater Outfitters Case Study: Part 1

Whitewater Outfitters is an apparel manufacturing and retail company specializing in upscale outdoor sportswear. The company supports multiple manufacturing plants in various sections of the country. The plants are considered to be silos; that is, each plant produces only certain specific lines of sportswear. Additional operations include retail stores in outdoor resort areas of the country and a very busy catalog sales business.

Each plant's manufacturing production is accomplished through production teams, which each have a leader who coordinates and assigns work. The team leaders run their production lines and are responsible for hiring, training, and managing the performance of their teams. All team members are cross-trained so that anyone can run any part of that production line.

Chris Martin is a training professional in the Davidson City plant. He is quite excited, as is the rest of the plant, about a recent announcement—Whitewater is adding a brand-new line of sportswear, called the City Slicker line. The new line will include men's, women's, and children's summer and winter apparel, shoes and boots, coats, and accessories. Much of the new line will be manufactured in the Davidson City plant.

Chris has been asked to come to a meeting with the plant production manager, Emerson Stewart, to discuss an upcoming training need. After greeting each other and settling in at the conference table, Emerson tells Chris some of the specifics about establishing the City Slicker line's production in the plant:

- The City Slicker clothing and accessories will be supported by three new production lines, which are scheduled to start up in six months.
- Some of the operations will be similar to those already in place in the plant, and a few will be new processes.
- The new lines will require hiring 50 new employees. New employees will be assigned to the City Slicker line or an existing team. In addition, some current employees will move to the City Slicker line; the rest will remain on their current teams.
- The hiring push for the 50 new employees will begin in three months.

Emerson concludes, "So you see, Chris, all the team leaders will be interviewing and hiring team members. We need to make sure we get excellent workers, not like some of the problem employees we've had lately. I want you to design and deploy a job interviewing skills class for the team leaders, and I want you to do it by the time the hiring push begins."

How should Chris handle the rest of this conversation? What questions should he ask Emerson? Write down your suggested questions here:

The main purpose of the initial conversation is to gain permission to conduct a needs assessment, which places a training request within the context of the organization's business needs and the client's business needs. It also anchors the job performance that is required to meet the business needs the eventual training program. Now that this permission has been obtained, it is time to plan the data collection for the needs assessment study.

3

Identifying Questions and Data Sources

 What's Inside This Chapter

This chapter helps you identify questions that must be answered by the training needs assessment. You'll learn about:

- the purposes of training needs assessment data collection
- why developing data collection questions, identifying data sources, identifying potential data collection methods, and choosing data collection methods should constitute four distinct thought processes
- common data collection questions
- characteristics of data sources.

3

Identifying Questions and Data Sources

The Purposes of Data Collection and Analysis

Training initiatives are designed to help employee-learners master knowledge and skills, which supports their increased job performance, which in turn supports the business goals linked to that performance. Training needs assessment is the foundation that guarantees the eventual training design and delivery hit the mark—at all four needs assessment stages (see Figure 1-1).

This chapter addresses the third step in the training needs assessment process: the point at which you collect data at needs assessment stages 2, 3, and 4 (performance needs, learning needs, and learner needs, respectively) to establish the need for training. Remember this book assumes you have entered the process near the end; that is, at the point where a potential training solution has been identified at step 5. Thus, your data collection process must take a few steps back so you can gather data to identify business needs for step 2. (Chapter 9 addresses following the needs assessment phases in the "right" order.)

Training needs assessment data collection serves multiple purposes; it:
- augments and validates the client's presenting business needs
- links the business needs to the client's goal and the desired training initiatives
- validates or refutes the hunches that came to you during the initial client conversation
- defines the business gap between current business needs and the desired business goals
- defines the performance gap between the current learner performance level and the desired learner performance level
- defines the knowledge and skills gap between the current learner skills and knowledge level and the desired learner skills and knowledge level
- identifies learners' needs in the learning environment.

Identifying the gap between actual and desired performance at each stage is critical to ensure that the eventual training design is tailored to bridge the gaps. Training that is designed to bridge performance and learning gaps adds value and, ultimately, positively influences the business.

Figure 3-1. The Training Needs Assessment Process With Step 3 Highlighted

Step 1. Conduct an External and Organization Scan

Step 2. Collect Data to Identify Business Needs

Capitalize on an opportunity
Resolve a problem
Support a strategy

Step 3. Collect Data to Identify Performance, Learning, and Learner Needs

Required performance
Learners' current performance
Required skills and knowledge
Learners' current skills and knowledge
Learner needs

Step 4. Analyze Data

Identify key data: gaps in performance,
skills, and knowledge
Identify recommendations

Step 5. Identify Potential Training Solution

Needed job aids and performance support materials
Types of training methods
Types of training delivery

Step 6. Deliver Data Analysis Feedback

Training recommendations: design and
delivery; ROI or ROE forecast
Nontraining recommendations: work
environment, rewards, consequences,
work processes

Transition Step: Begin Training Design

Think About This

By now you've noticed that the terms *employee* and *learner* seem to be used almost interchangeably. There is a pattern: When referring to employees in the organizational or business context, the term *employees* is used. When they are referred to in the training or learning context, the term *learners* is used.

 Noted

If a training request is geared toward learners who have no background or experience in the skills, measuring the gap by comparing current performance with desired performance is not necessary. Current performance is assumed to be zero, so data need to be collected only on desired performance.

4 Distinct Thought Processes

Planning your data collection consists of four separate thought processes:

- identifying the questions that must be answered by the data collection
- identifying the sources that can supply the required data
- identifying potential data collection methods
- choosing the data collection methods.

Why is it important to keep these thought processes and decisions separate? Too often a needs assessor says, "I will interview this person," or "I will conduct a focus group with these employees," and so on. In essence, this collapses the four thought processes—the question, source, potential method, and ultimate method—into one thought process, which results in prematurely identifying the data collection method you will use. Just as you wouldn't determine your training methods before you knew your training content and audience, you shouldn't determine your needs assessment methods before you know what data you will need and where to get them.

When you identify a method too quickly, you close down the creative thinking that is necessary for good data collection. What if, for whatever reason, that particular individual can't be interviewed or those people aren't available for a focus group? Because the question, data source, potential data collection methods, and ultimate data collection method were decided together, all four decisions become foregone conclusions. When one of those decisions cannot be implemented, the other three collapse with it. Whether you call it data collection tunnel vision, jumping to conclusions, narrowing the process too soon, or even thinking inside the box, it's very difficult to regroup and think about alternative methods. Because the initial thinking was limited by the realities of collecting the data, there is a distinct possibility that you will miss key questions and data sources in the earlier thought processes.

The initial thinking (identifying questions, data sources, and potential data collection methods) should not be limited by reality. Instead, keep the first three thought processes open. If you could ask any questions you wanted, what would they be? What would your data sources be if there were no constraints? When you get to the fourth decision, choosing data collection methods (chapter 5), you will be able to ground the data collection process in the limits of reality. Those limits will include time, cost, access to information, geography, available technology, and value of the data to the project. You will end up picking and choosing data collection methods that provide not only the most data, but the most useful data with a minimum expenditure of resources.

Some trainers become paralyzed by all the data or all the possibilities of the data. This is called "analysis paralysis." It is important to not be overwhelmed by the data. Instead, focus on identifying questions, data sources, and potential data collection methods in conjunction with your client to determine what will best help the organization overcome its current problems.

Basic Rule 5

Identifying data collection questions, identifying data sources, identifying potential data collection methods, and choosing data collection methods are four distinct tasks and thought processes.

Some trainers want to collect all the data that could possibly pertain to the training issue at hand. They become enamored of the data collection process because research is interesting to them. However, the purpose of needs assessment data collection is not research—it is to help the client "mobilize action on a problem" (Block 2000). This is what makes training needs assessment different from research. The main objective of data collection in training needs assessment is "action, not understanding" (Block 2000). Breaking down the choice of a data collection method into distinct thought processes results in a narrowing-down process that culminates in the selection of the best, most effective, and most efficient methods for the needs assessment project at hand.

The Data Collection Plan

Figure 3-2 presents a tool that is useful for organizing your data collection and for keeping your four thought processes separate. Write your data collection questions in the second column and insert a potential data source for each question in the third. List all data collection methods that could be used to address the question and access the source in the fourth column, and in the final column list the data collection method you chose. In this chapter, you will complete the second and third columns.

The data collection plan is a tool for you, not your client. When the plan is completed, you can transform the last column—your final data collection method—into a proposal or memo for your client, requesting permission to implement the methods and the necessary access. The plan then becomes your road map for implementing data collection. Later, it can also serve as part of the outline for your presentation of data analysis and recommendations.

Figure 3-2. Data Collection Plan

Data Collection Plan				
Project:				
Needs Assessment Stage	**Questions to Be Answered**	**Data Sources**	**Potential Data Collection Method(s)**	**Data Collection Method**
Stage 1: Business Needs				
Stage 2: Performance Needs				
Stage 3: Learning Needs				
Stage 4: Learner Needs				

Data Collection Questions

You must develop data collection questions based on your initial conversation with your client. What do you want to know at each stage—business needs, performance needs, learning needs, and learner needs? Table 3-1 presents some examples of targeted questions for each needs assessment stage, which you can customize to a specific data collection plan. Review this list and update it to help meet the needs of your projects. You won't need to ask every question for every project. Instead, find the ones that will answer the questions based on the need presented and the organization you are working with.

Table 3-1. Examples of Data Collection Questions

Needs Assessment Stage	Example Questions
Stage 1: Business Needs	• What problem(s) must be resolved? To what measurable extent? • What opportunity(ies) must be capitalized upon? What is the initial goal? • What strategy(ies) must be supported? What measures will indicate success? • What proportion of the problem, opportunity, or strategic goal will be attributed to the training effort?
Stage 2: Performance Needs	• What is a description of desired on-the-job performance? • What is a description of current on-the-job performance? • What are the specific gaps between desired and current on-the-job performance? • How is on-the-job performance measured? • How is on-the-job-performance managed and rewarded? • What tools and resources do the employees need to achieve the desired performance? • What is a description of the work environment in which the performance is expected? • What are post-training expectations for manager support for job application?
Stage 3: Learning Needs	• What do learners know now? • What can learners do now? • What skills do the learners need to be able to do differently? How well? • What do learners need to know to perform the skills? • What are implications in the work environment for transfer of learning back to the job? • Will training need to be delivered to new employees as they join the department, or it this a one-and-done training project?
Stage 4: Learner Needs	• What training have the learners already had in this area? • How did previous training go? • What is their attitude about the job performance that is being targeted? • What is their attitude toward the planned training program? • What organizational levels will the learners come from? • What will be the context in which they attend training (on the job, off the job, before or after shift, with their managers' support or not, arrangements made to be away from work, or expected to catch up on work during breaks)? • Will training attendance be voluntary or mandatory?

Identifying Data Sources

Now that you have developed some data collection questions, you need to identify a data source for each question. Remember, this is not about identifying the data collection method (for example, a focus group); it is about identifying the data source (for example, a specific group of people). This can be a tough distinction to make, so it can take some work to think about the data source apart from the data collection method.

Table 3-2 provides a list of potential data sources, the type of data that the source usually provides (by needs assessment stage), and advantages and disadvantages of each.

Table 3-2. Data Sources for Training Needs Assessment

Data Source	Type of Data and Needs Assessment Stage	Advantages of Source	Disadvantages of Source
Annual reports, benchmarking studies, sales figures, complaints, quality, customer satisfaction, productivity, HR data[1]	Business needs information (stage 1)	Data have already been collected and are easy to obtain; may need your client to provide access to the data source	Data were not collected for your purpose; you will have to extrapolate from the data to find indicators of the information you need
Upper management or client	Business needs information (stage 1)	Excellent source to discover the priorities of the business and what is really important	Access may be limited or even nonexistent as you go higher in the organization
Learners' managers	Desired performance (stage 2) Current performance (stage 2)	Can speak very clearly to the results and behaviors learners are expected to achieve on the job	Not necessarily cognizant of nontraining issues inherent in the work environment; may try to dictate what the training should look like; must keep on track to address performance only
Subject matter experts (internal or external, or resource materials)	Desired performance (stage 2) Desired knowledge and skills (stage 3)	Gives a clear picture of what performance looks like and what knowledge and skills it takes to get that performance	Cannot necessarily translate expertise into learning terms; training professionals must be able to do that
Job descriptions, performance evaluation data,[2] 360-degree aggregate data[1]	Current performance (stage 2)	Data have already been collected and are easy to obtain; may need your client to provide access to the data source	Data were not collected for your purpose; you will have to extrapolate from the data to find indicators of the information needed
Star performers	Desired performance (stage 2)	The best example of what excellent performance looks like because they do it every day	Performance may be so second nature that they can't identify components; needs assessor must do that
Customers	Desired performance (stage 2) Current performance (stage 2)	Gives clear picture of what customers want, which is a key performance driver; gives clear picture of what they are getting and their level of satisfaction	Customer feedback is without organizational context of performance expectations, logistics, and the feasibility of doing what they want
Learners	Current performance (stage 2) Learning needs (stage 3) Learner needs (stage 4)	Provides a great deal of information at multiple levels: what they do now, what they need to learn, how they need to learn	Sometimes uncomfortable with giving information and may give distorted data

Data Source	Type of Data and Needs Assessment Stage	Advantages of Source	Disadvantages of Source
Other training professionals	Learning needs (stage 3) Learner needs (stage 4)	Other trainers who have trained the target group can give information about skill levels and what learners need to learn, as well as on techniques and activities that work or don't work	Hard to tell how much of their feedback is influenced by their own training methods or biases
Previous training evaluation information[1]	Learning needs (stage 3) Learner needs (stage 4)	Gives information in learners' own perceptions regarding their learning needs and what works for them in the learning environment	Depth of information depends on when the learners filled out training evaluations; if it was in the last five minutes of a previous training course, the data won't have much meaning

[1] Data that already exist in the organization or external to the organization.
[2] Data are needed only in aggregate form because the goal is to identify performance of a group; individual data are neither necessary nor desirable.

It is clear that some sources can provide data at multiple stages of needs assessment. When data collection is designed and implemented, the methods must be carefully designed to cover all data needs in one collection effort. No source wants to be contacted multiple times just to be asked a few different questions each time!

Getting It Done

There are multiple challenges inherent in planning data collection for a needs assessment study. You must obtain permission from your client to gain access to data sources, and your client may have to obtain that access for you. Working with your client, identify the most critical questions to be answered and figure out how much data gathering you will need to do to get the answers. Nevertheless, it is important to remember that this is not a research study—it is a study regarding actions that must be taken.

Now, it's time to look in on Chris Martin to see how things are going at Whitewater Outfitters. Help Chris with step 3 of the needs assessment process by completing the first two columns of the data collection plan in Exercise 3-1.

Exercise 3-1. The Whitewater Outfitter Case Study: Part 2

In his meeting with Emerson Stewart, Chris Martin asked targeted questions to gain a clearer picture of the context surrounding the need for interview skills training for the team leaders. Table 3-1 lists some of the questions that Chris asked.

Emerson shared the following information about business needs:

- The team leaders must be ready to conduct interviews and begin hiring in three months.
- This plant's teams have an employee turnover rate that is 12 percent higher than the industry average. Emerson has heard through the grapevine that the employees who are leaving are going to jobs at Eddie Bean, another sportswear company plant on the other side of town.
- Complaints from retail store personnel and mail-order customers regarding poor-quality merchandise from this plant's existing product lines are currently at an all-time high, indicating there are production issues on the current lines.
- There have been four Equal Employment Opportunity (EEO) complaints from the production teams this fiscal year.

While Emerson wants the team leaders ready for the hiring push in three months, she also has other expectations that must be met in six months, after the new lines are up and running:

- lower turnover rates within the teams
- fewer complaints about poor quality from the retail stores and mail-order customers
- zero EEO complaints initiated by the teams.

Emerson's thoughts for performance needs are the following:

- All team leaders will have to interview and hire new team members from both internal and external sources, because all teams will lose some members to the new production lines.
- The team leaders as a group have poor interviewing skills, which lead to mismatched hiring decisions. These poor hiring decisions directly affect the high turnover that the plant is experiencing, because mismatched new hires leave quickly. If they are underqualified for the job, they quit due to frustration and stress; if overqualified, they quit due to boredom. Mismatched new hires also lead to quality complaints because employees who are not a good match for their jobs produce low-quality products.

- Team leaders are asking illegal interview questions that result in EEO-related issues and expose the plant and Whitewater Outfitters to legal liability issues and potential lawsuits.

Emerson thinks the skills the team leaders must perform better on (the learning needs) are:

- preparing for an interview
- conducting an interview
- asking legal interview questions
- making sound hiring decisions that lead to good new-hire matches with the job and job environment in the plant.

Emerson shared the following information about the team leaders as learners:

- The team leaders have never had any formal training on job interviewing skills in this plant. Therefore, whatever they are doing (right or wrong), they learned on their own.

By the end of the conversation, Emerson had offered to pave the way by sending introductory emails and allowing Chris access to the following people for data collection:

- Tracy Waddell, director of human resources
- Syd Diaz and Morgan Ciscyk, team leaders
- Riley Johnson, manager of the complaint center.

Chris knows that data collection involves assessing and validating the client's problems, as well as collecting additional data at all four needs assessment stages. What questions should he seek to answer in the data collection process? What data sources will answer these questions? Complete the second two columns of Chris's data collection plan (Questions to Be Answered and Data Source). Don't list data collection methods yet; you'll have a chance to do that in the next chapter.

Data Collection Plan				
Project: Interviewing Skills for Team Leaders, Davidson City Plant, Whitewater Outfitters				
Needs Assessment Stage	Questions to Be Answered	Data Sources	Potential Data Collection Method(s)	Data Collection Method
Stage 1: Business Needs				
Stage 2: Performance Needs				
Stage 3: Learning Needs				
Stage 4: Learner Needs				

Now that you've helped Chris begin a data collection plan for the needs assessment at White-water Outfitters, think about a training needs assessment project that you are working on right now, or one that you know you will be working on in the future. Re-create Figure 3-2 in a spread-sheet program, and use it as a template for current and future projects.

It may appear that step 3 in the needs assessment process is complete now that you have reached the end of this chapter. In truth, step 3 continues in chapters 4 and 5.

4

Evaluating Potential Data Collection Methods

 What's Inside This Chapter

This chapter offers guidance on how to choose data collection methods to answer the identified questions using the selected data sources. You'll learn:

- how step 3 in the needs assessment process continues with the collection of relevant data
- the difference between quantitative and qualitative data collection measures
- how and when to apply different types of analytical approaches for common data collection methods.

4

Evaluating Potential Data Collection Methods

Understanding Data Collection Methods

This chapter continues step 3 in the training needs assessment process (see Figure 3-1). In chapter 3, you examined the four distinct thought processes inherent in data collection, and developed your data collection plan. This chapter analyzes data collection methods for their uses, strengths, and weaknesses, so that potential methods for each data source can be identified. With that information in hand, you will be able to choose the optimal methods to implement for your situation.

Data collection methods are either qualitative or quantitative. Quantitative methods are those that result in hard data, which are objective and measurable, whether stated in terms of frequency, percentage, proportion, or time. Qualitative measures yield soft data, which are more intangible, anecdotal, personal, and subjective, such as opinions, attitudes, assumptions, feelings, values, and desires. Qualitative data cannot be objectified, and that is the characteristic that makes the data valuable. For example, knowing how job performers feel (qualitative measure) about a skill will be just as important in the ultimate training design as knowing how well (quantitative measure) they perform it.

 Noted

It is beyond the scope of this book to provide detailed instructions for implementing all potential needs assessment data collection methods. Instead, we provide explanations of the most frequently used methods and the basic how-tos. References to other sources for data collection are provided in the Additional Resources and References sections at the back of this book. Zemke and Kramlinger's 1982 book (a classic in the HRD field) provides very detailed and helpful information regarding how to implement specific (particularly quantitative) data collection methods.

Quantitative and qualitative measures can be combined in a data collection process for excellent results. For example, you can use a qualitative method (such as interviews) to collect anecdotes and examples. Then you can develop a quantitative method (such as a survey) using the collected anecdotes and examples as

Basic Rule 6

Both quantitative and qualitative data collection methods add value to the needs assessment process.

survey items and measure how many respondents fit the examples and how frequently the examples fit the respondents. Conversely, a quantitative method can be used first to collect information on the frequency and number of respondents. Then a qualitative method can be used to flesh out the survey items with richer detail. Qualitative and quantitative measures can also be combined in the same measurement tool. For example, items on a survey can be qualitative, such as feelings or opinions. How many times each item is chosen (frequency) is a quantitative measure.

Quantitative Data Collection Methods

Quantitative data, as we discussed, are hard data. They are usually gathered as statistics, numbers, and other objective data.

Extant Data

Existing records, reports, and data comprise extant data, which may be available inside the organization or external to it. Examples include job descriptions, competency models, benchmarking reports, annual reports, financial statements, strategic plans, mission statements, staffing statistics, climate surveys, 360-degree feedback, performance appraisals, grievances, turnover rates, absenteeism, suggestion box feedback, accident statistics, short-term and long-term leave records, customer complaints, quality statistics, production and labor costs, production rates, waste, rework rates, down time, late deliveries, repairs, training evaluation data, sales, pipelines, number of calls, time per call, time to sales, and competitive intelligence.

Extant data are often used for stage 1 and 2 measures for training needs assessment (business needs analysis and current performance analysis). Table 4-1 lists some advantages and disadvantages of using extant data for training needs assessment.

Table 4-1. Advantages and Disadvantages of Using Extant Data for Training Needs Assessment

Advantages	Disadvantages
• Hard data and measures • Can examine trends and patterns in the data over time • Consistent measurements provide reliable data • Does not involve individual employee confidentiality issues because data are used in aggregate form	• Usually collected for purposes other than training needs assessment, so training issues must be inferred from patterns in the data • No control over the methodology that was used to collect the data • Can be mixed in with data that are extraneous to your purpose so it must be "sifted" • Can be hard to get ahold of the data because other people control them • Data may be seen as sensitive and thus protected and need permission to use

Several methods are commonly used for collecting extant data. You can contact internal departments—HR, quality improvement, legal, finance, and so forth—that might have collected information that applies to the training need. Your client may have to make the request for you if the information is considered sensitive or the case needs to be made for why you need the data. You can also proactively scan the external environment by keeping up with business trends, company progress, regulatory issues, and current events. (Organization scans are discussed more fully in chapter 9.)

 Basic Rule 7

Information that will be useful in your situation and to your needs assessment purpose must usually be inferred from extant data.

Surveys

These are paper and pencil or electronic and email questionnaires that ask respondents a series of focused questions. Table 4-2 lists some advantages and disadvantages of using survey instruments for training needs assessment. Surveys are most often used for stages 2 and 4 measures for training needs assessment (performance analysis and learner analysis).

Table 4-2. Advantages and Disadvantages of Surveys for Training Needs Assessments

Advantages	Disadvantages
• Inexpensive • Results are easy to tally • Easy for respondents to participate • Gets quick results • Frequencies (how many respondents answered a question each way) are easy to understand • Can also be qualitative: Soft data questions yield qualitative data; the answer tally is quantitative	• It is challenging to construct questions that get the desired data in a configuration that meets your needs (must be careful with wording) • It is necessary to ensure that the wording of a question means the same thing to all respondents (reliability) and that the wording of the question will garner the information that is sought (validity) • Choosing an appropriate answer scale is critical • Respondents can skew the results by simply checking all one type of answer without really reading the questions • Sometimes can't get a large enough sample to make the data reliable (not enough people complete the survey)

When implementing surveys, it is important to formulate questions carefully to make sure they are clear as to interpretation. It's a good idea to pilot a survey with a small sample of the audience population to ensure that the items are unambiguous and that the survey has face validity and reliability.

Types of survey questions include yes/no, checklist, scaled (for example, on a Likert scale), forced ranking, and open-ended (completion of statements). You can even combine two rating scales for cross-referencing of data. Figure 4-1 is an example of a survey using two scales in this way.

 Think About This

In essence, reliability and validity are parameters that indicate whether a data collection method actually measures what it is supposed to measure. Specifically, a question or survey item is deemed reliable if it means the same thing to every respondent who answers the question and that the same respondents answer the question the same way if it is presented to them multiple times. Face validity means that the question appears to ask what it is intended to ask and it appears to be related to the needs assessment at hand. Construct validity means that the question accurately obtains the information that is sought. This is the purpose behind pilot testing a data collection method (say, a survey) with a small sample—to ensure reliability and validity of the resulting data.

Figure 4-1. Example of Using Two Ranking Scales on a Survey Instrument

Instructional Strategies Needs Analysis
For potential participants in train-the-trainer course

Please rank the following items twice on a scale of 1-5. The first ranking is the importance of this item to you, based on your job responsibilities (1 = not important at all; 5 = critical). The second ranking is a self-assessment regarding your level of knowledge (1 = I don't know very much about this subject; 5 = I am an expert in this subject).

Item	Importance (1-5)	Self-Ranking (1-5)
The experiential learning process and discovery learning		
Designing lectures		
Facilitating lectures		
Designing structured exercises		
Facilitating structured exercises		
Designing case studies		
Facilitating case studies		
Designing role plays		
Facilitating role plays		
Designing demonstration and practices		
Facilitating demonstration and practices		
Other types of learning activities (please write in)		
Setting up learning activities: grouping and instructions		
Designing activity debriefs		
Facilitating activity debriefs		
Adjusting facilitation on the fly to compensate for time, experience levels, hot issues, glitches		
Personalizing facilitation with stories, analogies, puzzles, and so forth		
Choosing media (flipcharts, handouts, PowerPoint slides, computer, video)		
Designing media		
Facilitating with media		
Developing facilitator guides		

 Basic Rule 8

Pilot test a survey with a sample of the intended population to ensure reliability in the meaning of the questions.

Assessments and Tests

These instruments gauge what the respondents know, can do, or believe in relation to the training need being investigated. Types of assessments include:

- knowledge assessments through verbal or written responses to multiple choice, true/false, fill-in-the-blank, or essay questions
- actual performance of a job skill while being observed
- analysis of work results, products, or outputs against quality criteria.

Assessments and tests are most often used for stages 2 and 3 measures for training needs assessment to gauge current learner knowledge, skill, or performance levels. Table 4-3 identifies some advantages and disadvantages of using tests and assessments for training needs analysis.

Table 4-3. Advantages and Disadvantages of Tests and Assessments for Training Needs Analysis

Advantages	Disadvantages
• Objective • Specifically identifies gap between current and desired performance, knowledge, and skills • Ultimate training design focuses on the specific gap rather than on generalized information	• Assessments don't always get to the thought processes behind why a participant performed in a certain way; accompanying with an interview can yield more complete data • Some participants can "freeze" and perform poorly due to test anxiety • Sometimes can be challenging to include both knowledge and skill tests and assessments due to time constraints in the training • Some participants won't complete the assessments in time (need to have a strong relationship with business partners to encourage completion and keep an open channel with the leaders when you aren't getting the number of results you expected)

It is critical to formulate questions and measurement criteria carefully to make sure they are clear as to interpretation when constructing a test. Consider using a test-writing expert to ensure validity beyond pilot testing if the content is highly technical or if you will be limited in using other methods to corroborate the needs assessment outcome. And, as is true with surveys, you should pilot the assessment with a small sample of the population to ensure face validity and reliability.

Basic Rule 9

Use a test-writing expert if assessments or tests are on highly technical subjects or if a test or assessment will be the sole, or one of very few, methods used.

Noted

The term *assessment* can also refer to instruments that measure frequency of behaviors, for example, a 360-degree feedback assessment or a commercially produced assessment of leadership behaviors used in conjunction with a model of leadership behavior. Such assessments can be produced internally or provided by external suppliers. The key is making sure that the assessment results provide information that will be useful in meeting the training need. Assessments can be used to gather others' perceptions of the targeted learners' behaviors or the learners' self-assessments of their own behaviors.

Job Task Analysis

This type of data collection involves a detailed examination (usually by interview and observation of a subject matter expert) of what it takes to do a job task, step by step. Job task analysis is most often used for analysis of desired performance (stages 2 and 3 measures). There are two main types of job task analysis: action-oriented or cognitive. Which type you need to perform will depend on your learners. If your learners primarily work with things, then you will focus on an action-oriented task analysis. If your learners primarily work with ideas and concepts, then you will focus on a cognitive task analysis. Some of the advantages and disadvantages of this data collection method are highlighted in Table 4-4.

Table 4-4. Advantages and Disadvantages of Job Task Analysis for Training Needs Assessments

Advantages	Disadvantages
• Best input into training design: provides content and materials that will translate into rich detail for learning activities that replicate the job environment and serve as a basis for skill and knowledge testing in the ultimate training course • Standards of performance included in the task analysis can be quantitative as well	• Subject matter expert who is acting as the data source must be seen as accurate and credible in the eyes of the organization • Time-consuming for the needs assessor to interview and observe the subject matter expert • Time-consuming for the subject matter experts to provide the information as they are going through the steps (they may think this process is long and tedious, so you need to reassure them of the value to the business)

Through a careful interview with and observation of the subject matter expert, the needs assessor can identify and document the following:

- the task
- the steps to complete the task

- performance standards (sometimes one standard for the entire task and sometimes several standards for each step) supporting task steps, knowledge, and attitudes necessary for successful task completion (eventually translated into enabling learning objectives during training design)
- resources necessary to complete the task
- description of the job environment
- job performance objective—a statement depicting what the task looks like on the job—which is eventually translated into a terminal learning objective in the training design process.

There are several methodologies for conducting task analyses. Figures 4-2 and 4-3 present two simple examples of a completed job task analysis. Figure 4-2 is a task analysis for an intellectual or cognitive skill ("develop legal interview questions"), and Figure 4-3 is for a physical or action-oriented skill ("hang a shower curtain"). Although hanging a shower curtain may seem a little silly as a task analysis, it is important that these examples represent skills that you are familiar with so you can see how steps and standards of familiar content are illustrated. If the content of the task analysis was unfamiliar to you, you could miss the linkages that are illustrated between steps and standards.

A simple way to conduct a job task analysis is to ask the SME to tell you the steps of a task. As the SME explains the steps, write down each one. Make sure to ask a lot of questions. You can work forward or backward so that you get the full view of each step in the task. (See the simple table in Table 4-5 for an example.) Ask the SME for step 1 to complete the task, then step 2, step 3, and so on until the task is finished. Once you've been given each step, ask the SME what knowledge or skill is needed to complete that step. When you're done with the list of steps, ask the SME what she does before she starts this task. Sometimes there are steps that the SME does automatically or doesn't consider part of the task. These could be important steps that people new to the job, or even average performers, don't know they need to do.

Then you can build out the full job task analysis including the performance standards, supporting materials, attitudes, and resources. See Figure 4-2 for sample performance standards for key task steps; in Figure 4-3, the performance standard refers to the entire task.

Table 4-5. Example Template for Determining the Steps of a Task

Step	Task	Skills Needed to Complete
1		
2		
3		
4		
5		
6		

Figure 4-2. Example of a Job Task Analysis for an Intellectual Task or Skill

Job Task Analysis: Interviewing Skills Course
Job Task or Skill: Develop legal interview questions.

Task Steps:
1. Analyze job description and resume and identify areas that should be examined in the job interview.
2. Make a list of specific items that should each have a specific interview question.
3. Draft an interview question for each item.
4. Assess each question for job-relevance and absence of illegal references.
5. Revise questions where applicable.
   – Standard: All questions are job related and contain no illegal references.

Supporting Knowledge:
• Review considerations in analyzing resumes.
• List the steps in the thought process that support the creation of legal, job-related questions.
• Describe EEO requirements that affect how organizations conduct job interviews.
• Differentiate between legal and illegal questions.

Supporting Attitude:
• Commit to preparing interview questions before the interview.
• Advocate developing questions that are both legal and job related.

Resources:
• Job description
• Job applicant's resume

Job Environment Description:
The environment is a stressful and rushed one in which it is difficult for learners to find quiet time to prepare for interviews. Consequently, they are tempted to wing it and form questions during the interview itself rather than beforehand, which results in a higher likelihood of illegal questions being used. Pressure exists to do this task correctly in light of previous legal problems.

Job Performance Objective:
Given a job description and an applicant's resume, develop interview questions that are job related and contain no illegal references.

Figure 4-3. Example of a Job Task Analysis for a Physical Task or Skill

Job Task Analysis: Training Course on Bathroom Decorating
Job Task or Skill: Hang a new shower curtain.

Task Steps:
1. Take the new curtain out of the plastic cover.
2. Shake the curtain out.
   – Standard: Fold lines and wrinkles begin to disappear.
3. Open the package of plastic hangers.
4. Place the hook of the first hanger in the hole at one end of the top of the shower curtain.
   – Standard: Little plastic filler dot in shower curtain hole has been removed.
5. Hang the curved part of the first hanger on the shower rod (use a stool to reach the rod if necessary).
   – Standard: The shower curtain design is facing out into the bathroom.
6. Repeat steps 4 and 5 until all the hangers are on the rod and the curtain is hanging.
   – Standard: The curtain is spread out over the length of the curtain rod.
7. Clean up all the little filler dots that have fallen into the bathtub.
   – Standard: All dots are removed.
8. Spray fragrance, or open a window, to rid the bathroom of new plastic odor.
   – Standard: New plastic odor is gone.

Supporting Knowledge:
- Describe the steps in hanging a shower curtain.
- Explain when to ensure that the shower curtain design is facing the appropriate direction.
- List two ways to rid a bathroom of new plastic odor.

Supporting Attitude:
- Advocate using a process to hang a shower curtain so that it is done correctly the first time.
- Commit to buying and hanging a new shower curtain whenever circumstances (guests, mildew) warrant the need.

Resources:
- New plastic shower curtain
- Plastic curtain hangers
- Shower rod
- Bathtub
- Stool (for shorter people to stand on when placing hangers on shower rod)
- Fragrance spray

Job Environment Description:
The bathroom can be a cramped area for this operation. In some bathrooms, the new-plastic odor of the shower curtain can be overpowering, so a fan or other form of ventilation might be needed. Short people will need a stool to reach the shower rod comfortably. For some people, reaching up to the rod repeatedly to attach the hanger is uncomfortable, and they might need short breaks. This can be a hurried operation in some instances (for example, guests are coming, or a shower is needed immediately).

Job Performance Objective:
Given a new plastic shower curtain, plastic curtain hangers, shower rod, bathtub, stool, and fragrance spray, hang a new shower curtain, so that the folds and wrinkles are beginning to disappear, little plastic filler dots have been removed from the shower curtain holes, the shower curtain design is facing out into the bathroom, the curtain is spread out over the length of the rod, all dots are removed from the bathtub, and the new-plastic odor is gone.

As you examine Figures 4-2 and 4-3, you might think, "This isn't how I would describe the task of developing legal job interview questions," or "This isn't how I would hang a shower curtain." That's because you are a content expert on these two skills (from your own background and experience), but you were not the content expert used as the source for these two task analyses! Often there are multiple ways of implementing a task correctly—particularly if it is a soft skill.

The "correct" content of a job task analysis is determined by the subject matter expert who provides the information (and the thoroughness of the individual needs assessor who conducts the task analysis). An SME can be an acknowledged expert in the field (internal or external to your organization), an employee who is a star performer in that skill, a reference source such as a book or other document, or even you—if you are an expert in the subject matter. What is important is that the SME is credible and that the SME's version of the task analysis is accurate in the eyes of your client and the organization.

You may need to do a job task analysis with a couple subject matter experts to make sure they are all doing the task the same way. If there is any difference between the SMEs and their methods of completing the task, talk with the client to determine which method is preferred for how they want everyone to perform the task. You must verify with your client that the job task analysis accurately represents the steps, standards, and environment for the job task before proceeding.

Qualitative Data Collection Methods

Qualitative data, as we discussed, are soft data. They are usually gathered as anecdotes, opinions, and other subjective reactions.

Interviews

You can use interviews—one-on-one discussions—to elicit the reactions of the interviewee on carefully focused topics. This data collection method yields subjective and perceptive individual data and illustrative anecdotes. It is most often used to collect data for stages 2 and 4 measures (current performance analysis and learner analysis) and is also used to gather business needs information from your client. Table 4-6 lists some advantages and disadvantages of interviews as a means for collecting data for needs assessment.

Table 4-6. Advantages and Disadvantages of Interviews for Training Needs Assessments

Advantages	Disadvantages
• Rich detail • Careful structuring of interview protocol produces consistent data across interviews that can be compared to identify patterns and trends • Can be used to flesh out quantitative data collected in a survey	• Can be time-consuming for the data gained • Interviewees must truly represent the targeted population or the data will be skewed • Frequency of responses does not get at the reason behind the responses (that is, why the respondents felt a certain way) • Interviewer must be careful to record interviewee responses, not interpret them

Interview questions must be planned ahead. You must structure the questions to garner the information that is most critical for your needs. Tips for conducting interviews include:

- Set the interviewee at ease. Begin with general questions and small talk. Slowly move into more specific questions.
- Use open-ended questions to get more detailed and rich data. Use closed-ended questions to control the interview and move on.
- Ask the interviewee to confirm and specify generalized statements and assumptions.
- Take notes. Use a page with interview questions already printed on it (an interview protocol; Figure 4-4) and make notes for each question. Show the interviewee your protocol and notes if asked.
- Allow pauses for the interviewee to think. Take a brief pause to complete your notes if necessary before moving on.
- You may wish to audio record an interview so that you can check back for the interviewee's exact wording when you are analyzing the data. If you choose to audio record, assure the interviewee that you are doing it to identify rich anecdotal phraseology and examples that might be significant for the study and for developing learning activities in the later training design. Tell the interviewee that his story will not be identified and that the recording will be destroyed after the study is complete.

 Think About This

When conducting interviews, you must differentiate confidentiality from anonymity. It is anonymity, not confidentiality, that you are promising to the interviewees. Assure interviewees that no one will know what each individual said and that the data collected will be used in aggregate and anecdotal form only.

Figure 4-4. Example of a Protocol for an Interview

Interview Protocol
For Potential Participants in Train-the-Trainer Course

Introductory Comments:

Thank you for allowing me some time with you to conduct this interview. Our time together should take ____ minutes *(longer time if in person; shorter time if on telephone)*. The data that I collect in this interview will be anonymous. That means that you will not be identified in any way by your comments. The comments will be used in aggregate form to identify trends in train-the-trainer needs. Specific comments may be quoted in reporting the data if they are particularly illustrative; however, the respondent will not be identified and any identifying information will be removed from the quotation. Even though I am recording the interviews, the audio recording is for my use only, so I don't miss anything when I take notes. When I am done transcribing our conversation, I will destroy the audio recording. Here's how we will proceed:

1. I will mention a train-the-trainer topic to you.
2. Please rate the topic first as to how important that topic is to your job. *(1 = not important at all; 5 = critical.)*
3. Then, please rate your own self-assessment regarding your current level of knowledge about the topic. *(1 = I don't know very much about this subject; 5 = I am an expert in this subject.)*
4. Last, for each topic, if you would like to add any comments, please feel free to do so.

Topics:

1. The experiential learning process and discovery learning
   • Importance ranking: _____
   • Self-assessment ranking: _____
   • Comments:

2. Designing lectures
   • Importance ranking: _____
   • Self-assessment ranking: _____
   • Comments:

3. Facilitating lectures
   • Importance ranking: _____
   • Self-assessment ranking: _____
   • Comments:

4. Designing structured exercises
   • Importance ranking: _____
   • Self-assessment ranking: _____
   • Comments:

5. Facilitating structured exercises
   • Importance ranking: _____
   • Self-assessment ranking: _____
   • Comments:

6. Designing case studies
   • Importance ranking: _____
   • Self-assessment ranking: _____
   • Comments:

7. Facilitating case studies
   • Importance ranking: _____
   • Self-assessment ranking: _____
   • Comments:

8. Designing role plays
   • Importance ranking: _____
   • Self-assessment ranking: _____
   • Comments:

9. Facilitating role plays
   • Importance ranking: _____
   • Self-assessment ranking: _____
   • Comments:

10. Designing demonstration/practices
    • Importance ranking: _____
    • Self-assessment ranking: _____
    • Comments:

11. Facilitating demonstration/practices
    • Importance ranking: _____
    • Self-assessment ranking: _____
    • Comments:

12. Other types of learning activities:
    _____
    • Importance ranking: _____
    • Self-assessment ranking: _____
    • Comments:

13. Setting up learning activities: grouping and instructions
    • Importance ranking: _____
    • Self-assessment ranking: _____
    • Comments:

14. Designing activity debriefs
    • Importance ranking: _____
    • Self-assessment ranking: _____
    • Comments:

15. Facilitating activity debriefs
    • Importance ranking: _____
    • Self-assessment ranking: _____
    • Comments:

16. Adjusting facilitation on the fly to compensate for time, experience levels, hot issues, and glitches
    • Importance ranking: _____
    • Self-assessment ranking: _____
    • Comments:

17. Personalizing facilitation with stories, analogies, puzzles, and so forth
    • Importance ranking: _____
    • Self-assessment ranking: _____
    • Comments:

18. Choosing media (for example, flipcharts, handouts, PowerPoint slides, or video)
    • Importance ranking: _____
    • Self-assessment ranking: _____
    • Comments:

19. Designing media
    • Importance ranking: _____
    • Self-assessment ranking: _____
    • Comments:

20. Facilitating with media
    • Importance ranking: _____
    • Self-assessment ranking: _____
    • Comments:

21. Developing facilitator guides
    • Importance ranking: _____
    • Self-assessment ranking: _____
    • Comments:

Closing Comments:
    • Thank you again for your time. The information you have provided will contribute greatly to an effective train-the-trainer course.
    • If you have any additional comments to share, please do so now.
    • You will see the results of this needs assessment. *(Provide an approximate date and explain how the information will be delivered, whether by the organization's newsletter, email, or some other means of communication.)*

Data collection interviews can be conducted over the telephone as well. Sometimes this is the only way to get an interview with someone who is hard to reach. Over the phone, you can conduct interviews with people who are far away, and you can use scripts, job aids, and so forth without the interviewee knowing.

Basic Rule 10

To be effective, data collection interviews must be carefully structured.

There are some disadvantages of telephone interviews. For example, you can't read the interviewee's body language, nor can you tell if the interviewee is distracted or doing something else (such as reading, typing, or driving) while you're trying to conduct an interview. Oftentimes, you also have less time to conduct a phone interview.

Critical Incident Interviews

During this specialized type of interview, the needs assessor asks the interviewee to tell stories about times when she felt effective or ineffective while performing the targeted skill. The stories are then analyzed for themes that provide indicators of behaviors that contribute to effective performance of the skill. This method is most often used for collecting data for stage 2 measures (desired performance analysis and current performance analysis). Some advantages and disadvantages associated with this method of data collection are listed in Table 4-7.

Table 4-7. Advantages and Disadvantages of Critical Incident Interviews for Training Needs Assessments

Advantages	Disadvantages
• Provides rich anecdotal data • Focuses on the critical behavioral differentiators of excellent performance so the ultimate training will be focused as well • Identifies skills and attributes that are not differentiators of critical performance, thereby supporting a tighter, streamlined training design	• Requires a great deal of time • Very expensive • Individuals who conduct the interviews and implement thematic analysis must be unbiased about what it takes to perform the skill effectively • Must use multiple thematic analysts to ensure reliability

For critical incident interviews, choose a sample of job performers, usually six to 10 individuals. You can focus on star performers (exemplars) if what is important is getting a complete picture of what excellent performance looks like. Or, you can choose two groups: star performers and some folks who are identified by the organization as average performers (although you would not tell them that). By using two groups, you can identify differentiating behaviors: those behaviors that only the star performers exhibit and are, therefore, the key contributors to excellent performance of the skill.

Conducting a critical incident interview is different from conducting a normal interview. Use an interview protocol (Figure 4-5) and begin by asking a general question such as, "What skills and knowledge do you think it takes to conduct job interviews effectively?" Although the rest of the interview must focus on capturing specific behavioral detail, opening with a general question helps the interviewee feel at ease. Then, for the remainder of the questions use a behavioral protocol: "What did you do?" "What happened?" "Why did you choose to do it that way?" Probe for behavioral details.

Although audio recording is optional in normal interviews, critical incident interviews must be recorded and transcribed. The exact phraseology is important in specifically describing the actual behaviors that were exhibited in a specific past event. Any time the interviewee shifts into generalizing or hypothesizing, steer her back into focusing on specific behaviors that she actually exhibited in the story she is telling. One sign that the interviewee has moved into generalizing or hypothesizing is the use of present tense. (When people tell a story about something that has occurred, they speak in past tense.) Phrases that signal generalizing or hypothesizing include:

- "I usually . . ."
- "Here at Whitewater Outfitters, we try to . . ."
- "I believe that . . ."
- "I'm the kind of person who . . ."

Figure 4-5. Example of a Critical Incident Interview Protocol

Critical Incident Interview Protocol
Interviewing Skills Training Course

1. What skills and knowledge do you think it takes to conduct job interviews effectively?
2. Tell me about a time when you think you did an effective job of conducting a job interview.
   (Prompting questions, as needed)
   – How did you know you had done an effective job?
   – What was the outcome?
   – How did you prepare? What did you do specifically?
   – What did you do to begin the interview?
   – What actions did you take as you conducted the interview?
     - What precipitated each action?
     - Why did you take the action?
     - What thoughts occurred to you as you chose each action during the interview?
   – How did you end the interview? What did you say and do?
   – What actions did you take after the interview? When? How?
3. Tell me about a time when you think you did an ineffective job of conducting a job interview.
   (Prompting questions, as needed)
   – How did you know you had done an ineffective job?
   – What was the outcome?
   – How did you prepare? What did you do specifically?
     - What parts of this are you satisfied with? Not satisfied? Why?
   – What did you do to begin the interview?
     - What parts of this are you satisfied with? Not satisfied? Why?
   – What actions did you take as you conducted the interview?
     - What precipitated each action?
     - Why did you take the action?
     - What thoughts occurred to you as you chose each action during the interview?
     - What parts of this are you satisfied with? Not satisfied? Why?
   – How did you end the interview? What did you say and do?
     - What parts of this are you satisfied with? Not satisfied? Why?
   – What actions did you take after the interview? When? How?
     - What parts of this are you satisfied with? Not satisfied? Why?

Basic Rule 11

To ensure reliability of data analysis of critical incident interviews, at least two individuals must be involved in conducting interviews, analyzing the transcripts, and identifying themes. Ideally, one analyst should be internal to the client's organization to provide context for behavioral examples; the other should be external to the client's organization to provide objectivity in analyzing responses.

Focus Groups

This data collection method is a group interview that provides rich data regarding the performers' or learners' job environment, current level of skill and performance, and their perceptions of desired skill and performance level. Focus groups can be used to collect information about stages 2, 3, and 4 measures (current performance, learning needs, and learner needs). Table 4-8 lists some advantages and disadvantages of focus groups.

It's important to conduct a focus group on neutral turf, for example, in a conference room that is not in the group's work area. When scheduling people to participate, be general: "We are going to talk about the challenges of conducting job interviews." Specifying the topic too closely ahead of time allows participants to prepare canned responses.

Table 4-8. Advantages and Disadvantages of Focus Groups for Training Needs Assessments

Advantages	Disadvantages
• Develops hypotheses that can be tested with a larger population through surveys or observation • The facilitator can make note of nonverbal behaviors that accompany statements • Skilled facilitation results in all focus group members being heard rather than just the more verbal participants	• Very time and resource intensive • Focus groups can fall under the influence of particularly verbal members and give the impression of unanimity when that's not necessarily the case • Difficult to facilitate with just one facilitator who must run the group and take notes • Focus group facilitators may find it hard to sit back and let the participants do most of the talking

Keep the size of a focus group to between five and 12 participants. Consider implementing multiple groups to get segmented data: a group of high performers, a group of average performers, and a group of performers' managers. When facilitating a focus group, use a focus group protocol (Figure 4-6), and move from general to specific questions. For example, start with, "How are job interviews conducted here at Whitewater Outfitters?" Gradually move to more specific questions: "In terms of legal or illegal interview questions, what are the trickiest areas, in your opinion?"

Figure 4-6. Example of a Focus Group Protocol

Focus Group Protocol
Interviewing Skills Needs Assessment

Introduction:
- Purpose of the needs assessment
- How the data will be used
- How and why you were chosen
- Ask permission to record the session
- Ask participants to introduce themselves, tell what part of the organization they work in, and how long they have been with the organization

Questions:
- How are job interviews conducted at Whitewater Outfitters?
- What do you think is effective in how interviews are conducted? What do you think is ineffective?
- What is your assessment of the outcomes of the interviewing process (that is, the quality of the new hires)?
- How did you learn to conduct job interviews?
- How do you prepare for conducting job interviews?
- What steps do you take in conducting an interview?
- In terms of asking legal and illegal interview questions, what are the trickiest areas?
- Once the interviewing process is over, how do you make hiring decisions?
- What parts of interviewing would you like to be able to do better? In what ways?

Use questions that encourage participants to speak up while you stay quiet as much as possible. Don't convey verbal or nonverbal communication about whether you agree or disagree with any statements offered by the participants, and don't interject your own comments.

 **Basic Rule 12**

Ensure that the data from focus groups will be worth the effort because this is a time-consuming and costly data collection method.

Make sure you document the data. Have someone take notes on flipcharts or paper (preferably not you because you have enough to do facilitating the group), or consider audio recording the conversation. If you decide to record the sessions, begin by offering assurances regarding anonymity and stating that the recording will be destroyed after it is transcribed.

Observation

This data collection method involves sitting with and observing star performers, experts, or average performers. More advanced versions of this method include time-and-motion studies and human factors studies—the tools of industrial engineers. In this method, an observer watches the job performer and documents each step that the performer implements in the performance of a task, including movements, amount of time for each step, and standards for successful performance. You can use observation to collect data on stage 2 measures (current and desired performance). Table 4-9 offers some advantages and disadvantages of this data collection method.

Table 4-9. Advantages and Disadvantages of Observation for Training Needs Assessments

Advantages	Disadvantages
• Excellent for assessing training needs for physical or psychomotor skills • Creates a step-by-step procedure (algorithm) that can be standardized for all learners in the form of a flowchart, diagram, graphic, list of steps, or job aid • If the observer notes job environment conditions that help or hinder performance, these can be included in the data	• Sometimes difficult to identify where a specific task begins and ends • Misses the performer's mental decision-making process at each step unless there is also an interview • Some performers may act differently than they would normally simply because they know they are being watched (known as the Hawthorne Effect); interviewing the performer after observation and asking why certain things were done in certain ways can help control for this effect

Observation accompanied by interviews can produce tools known as algorithms and help develop flow charts for a task. An algorithm depicts both physical steps and behaviors and the thought processes that support those steps. Figure 4-7 is an example of an algorithm depicting the skill of hanging a shower curtain. Notice that it includes both the steps and standards from the original task analysis, as well as patterns for internal decision making about the task steps. A flow chart shows the decisions that people must go through as they perform the task.

 Basic Rule 13

Observation reveals *what* and *how* performance should be implemented; accompanying observation with interviews identifies the *why* behind performance.

Don't Go Ballistic Over Statistics

You've probably noted in this chapter the use of terms such as *sample* and *population*, and you have been urged more than once to ensure that the audience sample you research is truly representative of the audience population. Does this mean that you might have to enter the scary realm of statistics and sampling techniques? Perhaps.

Figure 4-7. Example of an Algorithm Resulting From Observation

Algorithm for Hanging a Shower Curtain

Take a new curtain out of the plastic cover

Wrinkled?

YES

NO

Shake curtain until
wrinkles fall out.

Open the package of plastic hangers.

Are the little plastic "filler dots" removed from all holes in the curtain?

YES

NO

Remove all filler dots
from the curtain holes.

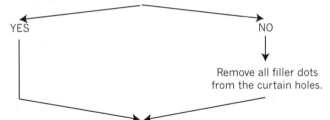

Are you tall enough to reach the curtain pole?

YES

NO

Get a stool and stand
on it.

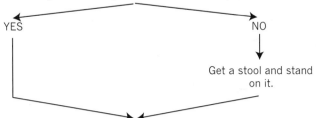

Hold curtain so that the designed side is facing outward, toward you.

Place the hook part of the first hanger in the first hole of the curtain.

Hang the curved part of the first hanger on the shower rod.

Figure 4-7. Example of an Algorithm Resulting From Observation (continued)

Evaluating Potential Data Collection Methods

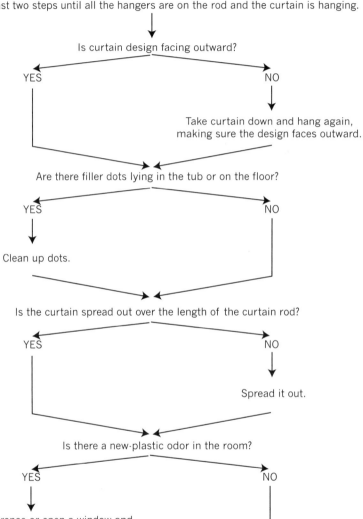

Repeat last two steps until all the hangers are on the rod and the curtain is hanging.

Is curtain design facing outward?

YES — NO

Take curtain down and hang again, making sure the design faces outward.

Are there filler dots lying in the tub or on the floor?

YES — NO

Clean up dots.

Is the curtain spread out over the length of the curtain rod?

YES — NO

Spread it out.

Is there a new-plastic odor in the room?

YES — NO

Spray fragrance or open a window and leave open until the odor is gone.

Finished.

If you are conducting a needs analysis for a small (one- or two-class) population and want to implement a survey, you'll be able to cover the entire population. For interviews, focus groups, or observation, you can ensure representativeness by drawing your subjects from differing work groups or backgrounds. Keep in mind that your training population is not a random representation of the organization's population because they all possess the selected common characteristic of needing the skills that will be taught in the training course.

Basic Rule 14

Be a good planner and consumer of statistical analysis—not a statistician.

If your training population is large (say, all first-line supervisors in a very large corporation, which could be anything from 100 to 10,000 people), you will want to implement sound statistical sampling techniques so you obtain representative data. There are references in the Additional Resources section that can assist you. Another suggestion, should you have need of moderately advanced (or in some cases, even basic) statistical analysis, is to hire a statistician or statistics graduate student to implement the statistics-related tasks in your needs assessment study. It is also possible, if you are working with a medium to large organization that there is someone on staff who can help you, who is an expert in the area of survey writing, focus groups, and statistical analysis. Your business partners would be able to help you find the resources. You can do it or you can find a business partner who can help you!

Completing the Data Collection Plan

To continue developing the data collection plan, the needs assessor identifies a potential data collection method for each data source and lists them in the potential data collection methods column of the plan. You may be given the data or names of data sources from your business partners. If they know the kind of data you are looking for, they may be able to tell you if the organization is already collecting the data. Or, as you are interviewing people and doing research you may discover that the data already exist, but no one related to this department knew about it. Because a training professional often works across departments, you may come across other types of data that are useful to your needs analysis. Sharing the data sources with your business partners is another way you can add value and build credibility.

When the data collection plan is complete to this point, it may appear that the data source and the data collection method are one and the same. This happens most often when referring to extant data. For example, if you are going to analyze data on absenteeism from the HR department, the item in the data source column will say something like "extant data on absenteeism from HR." The corresponding item in the potential data collection method column should say "analysis of extant data on absenteeism from HR." The two items are almost the same but not quite. The first item names the resource (person, department, report) that will provide the data; the second item describes what you will do to collect it, if you ultimately choose that method. If you find that two corresponding items in the two columns look exactly the same, one (or both) should be delineated more clearly.

When you've reached this point in your data collection plan, you will likely have many more methods in the potential data collection methods column of the plan than you can possibly implement. That is good; it means you have remained open throughout the thought process and have multiple methods from which to choose.

Another observation you may make as you wrap up the data collection plan is that data sources are repeated; that is, some data sources are listed more than once in answer to different data collection questions. Although this repetition may appear unnecessary, it is actually quite important: It guides you in identifying all the data you need from each source so you can prepare to collect all the data at one time from each source.

Table 4-10 summarizes all data collection methods described in this chapter and outlines their most common uses in needs assessment data collection.

Table 4-10. Summary of Data Collection Methods and Purposes

Method	Purpose	Quantitative or Qualitative
Extant Data	• Business needs • Performance needs	Quantitative
Surveys	• Current performance • Current knowledge and skill mastery • Learning needs • Learner needs	Quantitative
Assessments and Tests	• Current performance • Current knowledge and skill mastery • Perceptions of current knowledge and skill	Quantitative
Job Task Analysis	• Required performance • Required learning	Qualitative and Quantitative
Interviews	• Current performance • Learner needs	Qualitative
Critical Incident Interviews	• Required performance • Current performance	Qualitative

Method	Purpose	Quantitative or Qualitative
Focus Groups	• Current performance • Learning needs • Learner needs	Qualitative
Observation	• Required performance • Current performance	Qualitative

Getting It Done

Knowing the characteristics, advantages, and disadvantages of all the data collection methods available to you will help you identify the best potential methods for your needs assessment.

So, how are things going with Chris back at Whitewater Outfitters? The case study continues in Exercise 4-1.

Exercise 4-1. The Whitewater Outfitter Case Study: Part 3

First, take out the data collection plan you started in Exercise 3-1. Compare your data collection questions and data sources with the ones that Chris was able to identify in the data collection plan shown in Table 4-11. If you identified most of the same responses as Chris, congratulations! If you missed a few, go back to Exercise 3-1, work your way through the information in Chris's interview with Emerson, and see how Chris translated that information to the partial data collection plan shown here.

Now Chris must identify potential data collection methods, and while doing so must remember the caveat about not narrowing down the choices too soon. It is not yet the time to choose the methods that will be implemented. Use the information presented in this chapter to help Chris identify some potential data collection methods and list them in the column of the data collection plan (Table 4-11) under potential data collection methods. When you're finished, check your ideas against the next step of Chris's data collection plan in Table 4-12.

Chris knows that, practically speaking, not all these data collection initiatives can be implemented because of a shortage of time and resources (and Chris is only one person). Now he must decide which methods will provide the most useful data, and which methods will provide the most data at multiple needs assessment stages. In other words, which methods are optimal in terms of providing the best and most data with the least amount of resources committed? What methods should Chris choose from the potential data collection methods column? List your responses in the rightmost column of the data collection plan in Table 4-12.

Table 4-11. Data Collection Plan

Data Collection Plan			
Project: Interviewing Skills for Team Leaders, Davidson City Plant, Whitewater Outfitters			
Needs Assessment Stage	Questions to Be Answered	Data Source	Potential Data Collection Method(s)	Data Collection Method
Stage 1: Business Needs	a. What are the expected revenues for the City Slicker line? b. How much of the expected revenues is the interview skills training for team leaders expected to affect? c. How much of the current turnover can be attributed to the team leaders' current interviewing skills? d. How much of the retail store and customer complaints can be attributed to poor-quality products created by employees who are not good matches for their jobs because of poor hiring decisions and interviewing skills on the part of the team leaders? e. How many of the four EEO complaints in the current fiscal year are due to illegal interview questions? f. How do strong interview skills affect the business? How do they change or support the culture, company vision, and future of the work at the organization?	a. Emerson Stewart, client b. Emerson Stewart, client c. Tracy Waddell, HR, and HR extant data (e.g., turnover data, exit interviews, industry data) d. Riley Johnson, Complaint Center, Syd Diaz and Morgan Ciscyk, other team leaders e. Tracy Waddell, HR, and HR extant data f. Tracy Waddell, HR, and HR extant data		

Stage 2: Performance Needs	a. What is the required performance for effective interviewing? b. What does that performance look like? c. How do the team leaders currently conduct interviews? d. What is the team leaders' job environment like?	a. Tracy Waddell, HR b. Other "expert" HR staff, external HR resources (e.g., books, off-the-shelf training, other experts) c. Syd Diaz and Morgan Ciscyk, other team leaders, current team members who have been hired ir the last year d. Syd Diaz and Morgan Ciscyk, other team leaders
Stage 3: Learning Needs	a. What is the skill gap between team leaders' current performance and ideal performance? b. What skills and knowledge must the team leaders learn?	a. Expert HR staff, external HR resources (e.g., books, off-the-shelf training, other experts) b. Expert HR staff, external HR resources (e.g., books, off-the-shelf training, other experts)
Stage 4: Learner Needs	a. What are the team leaders' backgrounds in interviewing skills? b. What learning activities aid the materials best? How can the activities be presented so they're implemented on the job? c. How do the team leaders feel about the value that interviewing skills bring to this corporate strategy and hiring push?	a. Syd Diaz and Morgan Ciscyk, other team leaders b. Syd Diaz and Morgan Ciscyk, other team leaders, former instructors, extant data from former training evaluations c. Syd Diaz and Morgan Ciscyk, other team leaders

Table 4-12. Data Collection Plan

Data Collection Plan

Project: Interviewing Skills for Team Leaders, Davidson City Plant, Whitewater Outfitters

Needs Assessment Stage	Questions to Be Answered	Data Source	Potential Data Collection Method(s)	Data Collection Method
Stage 1: Business Needs	a. What are the expected revenues for the City Slicker line? b. How much of the expected revenues is the interview skills training for team leaders expected to affect? c. How much of the current turnover can be attributed to the team leaders' current interviewing skills? d. How much of the retail store and customer complaints can be attributed to poor-quality products created by employees who are not good matches for their jobs because of poor hiring decisions and interviewing skills on the part of the team leaders? e. How many of the four EEO complaints in the current fiscal year are due to illegal interview questions? f. How do strong interview skills affect the business? How do they change or support the culture, company vision, and future of the work at the organization?	a. Emerson Stewart, client b. Emerson Stewart, client c. Tracy Waddell, HR, and HR extant data (e.g., turnover data, exit interviews, industry data) d. Riley Johnson, Complaint Center, Syd Diaz and Morgan Ciscyk, other team leaders e. Tracy Waddell, HR, and HR extant data f. Tracy Waddell, HR, and HR extant data	a. Interview Stewart b. Interview Stewart c. Interview Waddell; analysis of extant data d. Interview Johnson; analysis of extant data; interview Diaz and Cisyk; interview team leaders; survey team leaders; focus group of team leaders e. Interview Waddell; analysis of extant data; survey of recent employee hires; survey of former employees f. Interview Waddell; analysis of extant data	

Stage 2: Performance Needs	a. What is the required performance for effective interviewing? b. What does that performance look like? c. How do the team leaders currently conduct interviews? d. What is the team leaders' job environment like?	a. Tracy Waddell, HR b. Other "expert" HR resources (e.g., books, off-the-shelf training, other experts) c. Syd Diaz and Morgan Ciscyk, other team leaders, current team members who have been hired in the last year d. Syd Diaz and Morgan Ciscyk, other team leaders	a. Interview Waddell b. Interview experts and resources; research resources c. Interview Diaz and Ciscyk; observe Diaz and Ciscyk; interview team leaders; focus group of team leaders; observe team leaders; survey recent new hires; interview recent new hires; analyze exit interview data (e.g., HR extant data) d. Interview Diaz and Ciscyk; observe Diaz and Ciscyk; interview team leaders; focus group of team leaders; observe team leaders
Stage 3: Learning Needs	a. What is the skills gap between team leaders' current performance and ideal performance? b. What skills and knowledge must the team leaders learn?	a. Expert HR staff, external HR resources (e.g., books, off-the-shelf training, other experts) b. Expert HR staff, external HR resources (e.g., books, off-the-shelf training, other experts)	a. Interviews, research b. Interviews, research

Table 4-12. Data Collection Plan (continued)

Needs Assessment Stage	Questions to Be Answered	Data Source	Potential Data Collection Method(s)	Data Collection Method
Stage 4: Learner Needs	a. What are the team leaders' backgrounds in interviewing skills? b. What learning activities aid the materials best? How can the activities be presented so they're implemented on the job? c. How do the team leaders feel about the value that interviewing skills bring to this corporate strategy and hiring push?	a. Syd Diaz and Morgan Ciscyk, other team leaders b. Syd Diaz and Morgan Ciscyk, other team leaders, former instructors, extant data from former training evaluations c. Syd Diaz and Morgan Ciscyk, other team leaders	a. Interview Diaz and Ciscyk; observe Diaz and Ciscyk; interview team leaders; focus group of team leaders; observe team leaders b. Interview Diaz and Ciscyk; interview team leaders; focus group of team leaders; observe team leaders; analyze past training evaluation data c. Interview Diaz and Ciscyk; interview team leaders; focus group of team leaders; observe team leaders	

It's time to shift from Whitewater Outfitters back to your own organization. Go back to the photocopy or spreadsheet you made of Figure 3-2, where you have already listed your data collection questions and your data sources for a training needs assessment project you are working on right now, or one that you will be working on in the future. List some potential data collection methods in the next column. You'll have a chance to select your final data collection methods and complete the plan in the next chapter.

Now that you have completed three of your four critical data collection decisions, it is time to choose the data collection methods that you will implement.

5

Data Collection Implementation

 What's Inside This Chapter

This chapter offers guidance in the ultimate choice of data collection methods. You'll learn:

- factors that assist you in choosing the most effective data collection methods for your needs
- tips for implementing data collection
- why collecting data from multiple sources and at multiple stages is critical to your ultimate training design.

5

Data Collection Implementation

Choosing Data Collection Methods

Another critical part of step 3 of the data collection process is choosing (from the list in the potential data collection methods column of your data collection plan) the data collection methods that will work best in your situation to gain optimal information. You should choose both quantitative and qualitative methods so that your data sets complement one another. There are several factors that you should consider in making data collection method choices. Some important ones are described in Table 5-1.

Basic Rule 15

Choose both quantitative and qualitative data collection methods.

Table 5-1. Some Factors to Consider When Selecting Data Collection Methods

Factor	Considerations
Time Needed	• What is the timeframe for your data collection process? How quickly must the training be designed and implemented? • How much time do you have available to conduct the data collection, keeping in mind your other commitments? • How much time does each data collection method take to implement?
Other Resources Needed	• How much of other employees' time will be needed to assist in actual data collection for each method? • How much of other employees' time will be needed as subjects of each data collection method (e.g., interview subjects, survey respondents, and so forth)? • What commitments in terms of other organizational resources (e.g., clerical time, equipment, tools, disruption of the work process) are necessary for each method?
Other Costs	• How much will it cost to buy equipment, software, assessment tools, and so forth to implement a particular data collection method? • Are there any fees for external services for conducting interviews, inputting data, transcribing tapes from interviews or focus groups, carrying out statistical analysis, or other activities? • Are there travel expenses necessitated by implementing the selected data collection method?

Factor	Considerations
Essentialness	• Is a specific data collection method one of only a few (or perhaps the only method) that can obtain a needed data set? • Could other data collection methods yield the same data?
Availability of Data Sources	• For each data collection method, which data sources will be easy to access (i.e., extant data or people are easily obtained)? Which sources will take time and resources to gain access? Is appropriate leverage from the client available to assist in gaining access to? • Are there internal political implications that apply to certain methods or data sets? • What time of year or part of the organization production cycle is it? Access to people, data, and the work environment can be limited if it is the organization's busy season or if it is a time of year when people are away (e.g., vacations and holidays). • How willing is your client to help you gain access to data sources for each method? (For example, a client may be more willing to allow an email survey than a series of interviews due to perceived disruption of work.)
Logistics	• Are data sources located at multiple sites? Will you have to travel to gather data? • How essential are the data collection methods that require travel? Would another method suffice? (For example, can you conduct telephone interviews with people who are at other sites rather than conduct them face-to-face?) • Is there technology (e.g., email or videoconferencing) available in the organization to assist with logistical issues? If so, will you need assistance in managing the technology or do you already know how to use it? • Is there appropriate space in the organization to conduct each data collection method (for example, a private room for interviews, a place to observe work without being intrusive)?
Needs Assessor's Skill Level	• Are there some methods in which you have more experience and expertise? When you have a choice of methods, it can save time and resources to use a method that you know and can do well.

Here are a couple of thoughts about Table 5-1. First, the concept of essentialness regarding data collection methods is about the uniqueness of the data that a particular method offers you. It does not mean the same thing as the importance or significance of the data being collected. For example, job task analysis would be considered highly essential because it provides data on performance standards (how well each step of a task should be completed)—and very few data collection methods do that. An interview would be considered a less essential method because some of the same data can be obtained from a survey or focus group.

Second, the table indicates that the needs assessor's skill level is another factor to consider, but it is a double-edged sword. If you have expertise and are comfortable with using particular data collection methods, you can probably apply them quite efficiently. But, there is also a downside to using only data collection methods in which you have expertise. You've probably heard the expression, "When you get a new hammer, everything in the world looks like a nail." That's what can happen when you continue to choose only data collection methods that you are most familiar with. It becomes very tempting to use the same methods over and over, even when they might not be the best choices. If you reach an unbiased conclusion that a method in which you have little expertise is the best one for the need, it's time to learn how to implement that method. Take the time to teach yourself, seek training that will help you learn it, or hire an expert and shadow that person to learn how to implement that data collection method. The extra effort spent will be worth it.

Third, remember to collect only data that you will actually use. Training needs assessment is not the same as pure research. Your job is to help the client take action to resolve a problem, capitalize on an opportunity, or support a business strategy. Collect enough data to ensure that the ultimate training solution will support the client's ability to take appropriate action.

In Table 5-2 you see the column for resources needed and for other costs. There is a real cost to each method of data collection. You need to find the balance between getting the data you need, within the time you need it, and within the needs assessment budget you were given, if you were given a budget. Sometimes the cost for a data collection method is the time you take people away from their jobs to interview them or hold a focus group. This is a real cost to the business that must be respected and considered as part of your data collection plan.

 Basic Rule 16

Choose to implement data collection methods that will get you the best data with optimal expenditure of resources. Consider time, other resources, financial costs, essentialness, data source availability, logistics, and your own skill level.

Table 5-2 provides a summary of the criteria above as they apply to the most commonly used data collection methods. As you examine the table, you'll likely notice an interesting paradox: In many cases, a data collection method that provides highly essential data also requires great expenditures of resources in terms of time, money, person-hours, or other resources. Conversely, methods that tend to provide less essential data usually require lower resource expenditures. Does this mean that you should only choose methods that provide highly essential data? No. First, remember that in this context, the essentialness of a data collection method means how unique the data collected are; it does not signify the importance of the data. Second, even if you wanted to do so, you don't have the resources to implement all the "essential" methods for one project! So, judiciously select one or two essential (and resource-consuming) methods and augment these with less resource-intensive methods.

Table 5-2 compares the feasibility of data collection methods across the selection criteria discussed in this chapter. Note that the rightmost column labeled "Needs Assessor's Skill Level" is blank. That must be filled in by the individual needs assessor.

Review your data collection plan with your client to make sure he is aligned with and has signed off on your plan. The client will be the one held responsible for the costs and the time lost during the training needs assessment. If the client isn't aware of the data collection plan or hasn't approved it, this could jeopardize your relationship with him, your credibility, and the credibility of the training department at your organization.

Table 5-2. Criteria for Choosing Data Collection Methods

Listed below are data collection methods and high, medium, and low rankings for their feasibility across the selection criteria discussed in this chapter. Note that the rightmost column labeled "Needs Assessor's Skill Level" is blank. That must be filled in by the individual needs assessor.

Data Collection Method	Time Needed	Other Resources Needed	Other Costs	Availability of Data Sources	Logistics	Essentialness of Data	Needs Assessor's Skill Level
Extant Data	Low	Low	Low	High	Medium	Medium	
Surveys	Medium to High[1]	Medium to High[3]	Medium to High[2]	Medium	Medium	High	
Assessments and Tests	Low	Low to High[4]	Low to High[4]	High	Low	High	
Job Task Analysis	High	Medium	Low[5]	Medium	Low	High	
Interviews	Medium to High	Low	Low	High	Low[6]	Medium	
Critical Incident Interviews	High	High	High	Medium	Low	High	
Focus Groups	High	Medium	Low	Medium	Medium	Medium	
Observation	High	Low	Low	Medium	Low	Medium	

[1] Medium to administer; high to analyze.
[2] Depending on whether other resources must be used to design, enter data, or conduct statistical analysis.
[3] Depending on whether resources to design, enter data, or conduct statistical analysis must be purchased.
[4] Low if assessment or test already exists; high if assessment or test must be constructed.
[5] Medium if external job analyst is hired.
[6] Can be high if subjects are geographically dispersed; consider telephone interviews instead.

Implementing Your Data Collection

At last you are finally ready to collect your data. Here are some tips to help you implement the process efficiently and effectively.

- **Double-check.** Make a last quick pass over your choices and your reasons for choosing each method. Don't be afraid to make last-minute adjustments before you get started. It is important to be sure you have chosen methods that will optimize your time, access to resources, and the ultimate value of the data, as well as conforming to the budget and time constraints for the project. Review any changes with the client before you implement the updated plan.

- **Make a plan.** Develop a calendar, timeline, flowchart, or some other tool to help you stay on track and remind you that you have a deadline to complete the data collection. Put each data collection method on the timeline or spreadsheet, determine how much time you think each task will take, and calculate whether you have enough time to complete each data collection task. If not, adjust your schedule or your methods. Monitor your progress on the plan as you go along so you can stay on track, communicate your progress with the client, and meet your client's deadlines.

- **Be flexible.** One of the nice things about having a plan is that you'll know when you must deviate from it. Accept the fact that things happen in organizational life that are out of your control, and prepare to adjust your data collection as you go along. Did one segment take longer than you thought it would, causing you to implement another segment more quickly than you planned? Are there alternative data collection methods that can be used if it turns out that the one you selected isn't feasible? Are there other people on the training team who can help you with some of the data collection? Can people without access to email receive a paper survey? Also, try to implement the most essential methods first, in case circumstances force you to cut the data-gathering process short.

- **Include your client regularly and frequently.** Remember, your client must approve your data collection plan, budget, and timeline before you start. Then, you must also report back to the client periodically about your progress. It doesn't have to be a formal report; even a voicemail message or email will do. By keeping in touch with the client, if you must change your plan due to organizational circumstances, the client will know about it and can help you get access to alternative data sources. By sharing tidbits of information gathered along the way, you can pique the client's interest in the process and the eventual results, demonstrate the value in the process, and build your credibility. Finally, if you discover data items that are contradictory, the client can help provide context and meaning.

- **Keep your own interpretations and experiences out of the data collection.** This is a critical caveat. Your data must be objective or your ultimate data analysis will not be accurate. There are many points at which it is tempting to augment the data with your own views; for example, you try to "help" an interviewee by interpreting what is said by saying something like "So what you really mean is . . ." rather than saying "Can you tell me more about that?" Resist the temptation to add your two cents' worth.

- **Be objective.** Avoid structuring data collection to play on your hunches. For example, you get a hunch during an initial interview with a client that part of a performance problem is obsolete equipment. Asking a question in an interview or survey like "What problems have you had with equipment?" is leading and plays too closely on your hunch. Instead, a better question might be "What keeps you from achieving the results that are expected of you?" If part of the problem is obsolete equipment, it will come out. Your opportunity to test hunches is in data analysis, not data collection.

- **Use extant data correctly.** It's already been said that extant data are rarely if ever collected for your purposes, so you must infer from those data and take steps to validate the inferences if necessary. For example, if many employees said in exit interviews that one of the reasons they left the organization is that the company's benefits program isn't as good as other companies', this is important information. However, it isn't necessarily true information. It means that many of the employees who left believe that it's true. Check it out with another data source, or address it in your recommendations (chapter 7).

- **Use others to achieve reliability.** If possible, involve other people in some of the data collection to help control for any bias you might have. Have others conduct some of the interviews or take a look at extant data. You can use co-workers from the training or HR department, or your client may provide access to a manager who has an interest or stake in the project.

- **Plan how you will share the data when data collection is complete.** Work with your client to decide how the data will be shared with the sources who cooperated with you in the data collection process. To build your credibility and your value as a trusted business partner, it's important to share your data with the people from whom you collected it. You and your client have the prerogative to decide what data and how much of it to share, but some kind of follow-up must happen or your credibility can be damaged.

- **Skim or sample the data as they are being gathered.** If any unique or significant information appears, there is still time to focus subsequent data collection on validating that information or on gathering more of it. Have a discussion with the client about it to confirm the need to gather more information or make changes to the data collection plan based on the new or significant information.

- **Stop when you get repetitive data.** There's no rule that says you must complete all the data collection methods in your plan. It has already been mentioned that you might have to cut data collection short because of circumstances. You can also stop when the data trends become so clear that it is likely that more data will simply provide the same information. If the first 10 interviewees said the same thing (and your sample is representative), the last five interviewees will probably say the same thing as well.

 Noted

What if you want to collect data at multiple stages from the same source? Say, for example, you know that from a sample group of learners you can gain information about their current skills, what they would like to do better in terms of their job performance needs and learning needs, and their availability for attending training (such as geographical restraints). Does that mean you have to conduct three focus groups with them or implement three surveys? No. Develop all your questions for the focus group or survey and administer them all at the same time. Not only is that more efficient for you, but it is more efficient for and respectful of your data sources as well.

The Ultimate Goal: Generating the Training Design

Chapter 1 discussed three purposes of training needs assessment:

- Training needs assessment places the training need or request in the context of the organization's needs.
- It validates and augments the initial issues presented by the client.
- It ensures that the ultimate training design supports employee performance and thereby helps the organization meet its needs.

Chapters 1 and 2 presented more detailed discussion regarding the first two purposes of training needs assessment. It is now time to discuss the third purpose, that of ensuring that the ultimate training design will support employee learning and job performance. How exactly does the training needs assessment serve as an input for the ultimate design? What does each stage of needs assessment specifically add to the training design? The following sections address how each stage of a needs assessment feeds into the training design and offers some examples of how one organization (a hospital) designed training around needs assessment.

 Think About This

One of the struggles faced by all authors of the books comprising ATD's Training Basics series is identifying where to draw the line between the subject matter of one book and the subject matter of a related book. It is a struggle because in the real world of training, all the processes—needs assessment, design, development, delivery, and evaluation—are part of a system in which all these components are interdependent. At times, it is necessary to address when and how one component of the system depends on another component. The discussion in chapter 1 regarding how needs assessment and evaluation are related was one of those instances. This discussion of how needs assessment fits into training design is another.

Stage 1: Business Needs Data

How do data about the needs of a business support the ultimate training design? When a client makes a training request, it is important to frame that request in the context of business needs. Chapter 1 discussed how that process is important to the training function and to the organization. It is also important for the ultimate training design.

Using Stage 1 Data in Training Design

You'll recall that business needs involve resolving a problem, capitalizing on an opportunity, or supporting a strategy. The most common sources of information about the needs of the business are the client, other leaders of the business, and extant data. Business needs are included in the ultimate training design in the following ways:

- The needs of the business can be used in the introduction of a training course to anchor the course in the realities of the environment and the business and to give the learners the big picture about why they are in the training course.
- If learners must be encouraged to buy into the training course, you can help motivate them by providing specific statistics on how increased performance (based on the

training course) will affect the business and by how much, and thus help them be more productive and successful.

- Statistics and scenarios that show the business need can be built into learning activities (case studies, discussions) to make the course relevant and allow the learners to apply their learning to the actual business. Adult learners need the training to be relevant to their work. By placing the learning in the context of the work, the learners get a chance to try the new skills in a safe environment, and practice what they will eventually do back on the job.

Example

A local hospital has identified a training need to increase patient interaction skills of nurse's aides in all units related to maternity services (this includes not only the maternity department, but also OB/GYN care, prenatal services, and women's informational and public service events and efforts). There are two business needs driving the training need. First, patient satisfaction statistics in maternity-related areas are slipping (a business problem to resolve), and second, another local hospital has closed down its maternity services, so a prime opportunity exists to become the community's "baby hospital" (a business opportunity to be capitalized upon).

Business needs data provide input into the ultimate patient interaction skills training course design in several different ways. Here are some examples that might be recommended based on the data collected, but you may be able to think of others:

- an introductory learning activity in which the strategic plan for becoming the community baby hospital can be presented
- sharing of patient satisfaction statistics with a subsequent learning activity regarding generating ways to increase those figures
- scenarios or cases that depict interacting with patients in a way that promotes the hospital's baby-related services
- developing or sharing a "patient interaction chain of events," beginning with the planning for pregnancy and ending with postnatal services, which demonstrates all the opportunities the hospital and the learners have to maximize individual patient satisfaction and promote future use of the hospital for maternity-related needs by that patient and all of her contacts (potential hospital customers).

Stage 2: Performance Needs

How does identification of job performance needs data support the ultimate training design? Collecting and identifying data regarding performance needs focuses on what the learners will ultimately have to do back on the job. These data provide information on task steps that employees must perform, the work environment in which they perform, and quality standards for the results they achieve. This information is critical because an effective training design must replicate as closely as possible the skill as it is performed on the job.

Performance needs information must be collected along two lines: What does desired performance look like? What does current performance look like? For desired performance, the most common sources of performance needs information are the client or the managers of the employees, star performer employees, SMEs, and extant data. For current performance needs, the most common sources are the current job performers, the employees' managers, and extant data.

Using Stage 2 Data in Training Design

By comparing the two sets of data on desired and current performance, you can identify the specific performance gap that must be addressed by the training. Identifying this gap is also critical because when training focuses on bridging the performance gap it takes less time by focusing on what the learners really need, the learners are more likely to value the training, the ultimate job performance improves because the true performance gap was addressed, and morale problems associated with irrelevant training are avoided. Sometimes there is a gap because you are introducing a new product or a new system or machine. Sometimes there is a gap because the employees aren't executing correctly or completely on tasks they are already supposed to be performing. How you solve for a performance gap is different from how you solve for a new product or system gap.

Job performance needs data are included in the ultimate training design in the following ways:

- basis for learning objectives for training design
- specifics regarding the performance gap to be addressed
- on-the-job performance measures that will be translated into tests and assessments in the training design
- indicators for the depth at which to treat knowledge and skills in the training design (identifies which training content can be treated at the knowledge level only and which content must be taken to the skill level in terms of practice and application)

- simulation of the job environment for learning activities (for example, tools, working conditions, job environment)
- indicators for transfer learning strategies
- evaluation methods and measures will be identified as the job standards are developed.

 Think About This

Transfer learning strategies are ways of designing and delivering training that encourage application of the learned skills back to the job environment. Reproducing the job environment as closely as possible in the classroom is a transfer strategy: If learners practice a skill in a classroom environment that is very similar to that in the workplace, they are more likely to have confidence in their ability to perform the skill back on the job and, therefore, are more likely to choose to use the skill. Other examples of transfer learning strategies might include action planning for back on the job, or identifying barriers to using the skills in the workplace, and then strategizing tactics to overcome the barriers.

Example

Continuing with the hospital example: Job performance needs assessment data collection regarding the patient interaction skills training course for nurse's aides revealed two specific job performance gaps in this group of employees. First, their job environment is very fast-paced and stressful; they are often interrupted when caring for or interacting with a patient. Consequently, they become distracted and fail to continue the patient interaction or follow up with them. Second, the nurse's aides don't feel capable of handling patient complaints when the patient is upset or angry; instead, they usually refer these issues to their supervisors. Because it takes time for the supervisor to contact the patient and review the complaint, the result is often intensified patient dissatisfaction because of the delay and suboptimal use of the supervisor's time.

With this information in hand, the training design of the patient interaction skills training course might focus on the following components:

- presentations on the costs related to patient dissatisfaction and referrals of "escalated" patient complaints to supervisors
- role plays in which interactions between a nurse's aide and a patient are enacted and interrupted, accompanied with strategies and job aids to support nurse's aides' skills in handling the interruptions efficiently, and in remembering to follow up to continue a patient interaction when it is interrupted

- skill-based training on handling conflict situations to include steps in handling conflict, scripts for handling the most common patient complaints, and role plays that provide opportunities to practice the skills
- a learning activity that focuses on why it's hard to handle conflict with a patient and why it's important to choose to do it
- transfer strategies that include a job aid (laminated card) containing the conflict handling steps that nurse's aides can refer to on the job and a follow-up brown bag luncheon in which nurse's aides share their experiences, get advice, and celebrate their accomplishments in handling situations more effectively.

Stage 3 Data: Learning Needs

Data regarding learning needs focus on what the learners must learn in the classroom to perform as required on the job. Much of this information is similar to job performance data in that it includes task steps that employees must perform, the work environment in which they perform, and quality standards for the results they achieve. The difference here is that learning needs reflect how the skills must be learned, rather than how they must be performed on the job, and how the skills must be performed in the learning environment to master the skills in the job environment.

Learning needs also focus on the gap—only this time, it is the gap in learning rather than in performance. What must the learners *know* in order to *do*? Some of the same data sources are consulted for learning needs as in performance needs: For learning that is required, SMEs, extant data, and star performers are the most common sources. For current learning level, the current job performers are the main source of data, which can be augmented with extant training evaluation data from other courses.

Using Stage 3 Data in Training Design

Learning needs data supports the ultimate training design because it:

- translates learning objectives into learning activities
- provides content for knowledge-based learning activities
- provides test and skill assessment items for measurement of learning in the training course, based on how the knowledge and skills are exhibited on the job
- helps identify the depth and time that should be allotted to each knowledge and skill activity, based on importance.

Example

Learning needs assessment data collection regarding the patient interaction skills training course for nurse's aides revealed, among other things, that:

- There are specific steps to follow in handling a complaint situation that help in resolving it and in lessening the possibility of escalation.
- An interpersonal skill set is associated with handling conflict and complaint situations.
- The nurse's aides feel like they are winging it every time they handle a complaint.
- The better a nurse's aide is at handling interruptions, the more satisfied the aide's patients are.
- The more their co-workers interrupt them, the more stressed the nurse's aides feel.

With this information in hand, the training design of the patient interaction skills training course might incorporate the following activities:

- knowledge-based activities on handling co-worker interruptions
- knowledge-based activities and job aids on the steps for handling a conflict interaction
- knowledge-based activities on when to escalate a complaint situation to a supervisor
- skill-based activities (role plays) on handling interruptions from co-workers
- skill-based activities (role plays) that provide practice both in handling complaints from patients and in handling interruptions from co-workers (the same role plays as mentioned in performance needs analysis with an additional layer of content added based on stage 3 data)
- knowledge test items that reflect job application (for example, nurse's aides often use a reference manual as a regular part of their daily work; in a test in the classroom, they should be "looking up" items in the manual as well; forcing them to answer from memory does not reflect how it's done on the job)
- a short segment on stress reduction techniques (deep breathing, for example).

Stage 4 Data: Learner Needs

Data regarding learner needs focus on how to make the learning environment conducive to learning for a specific group of learners. The current job performers are the main source of data, with some contributions from extant data in the form of prior training evaluation information.

Using Stage 4 Data in Training Design

How does identification of learner needs data support the ultimate training design? Learner needs data provide the following input into the training design:

- learning activities that are most conducive to the specific learners and the job duties of the learners
- pace and energy level of the training (based on time of day and time in learners' work cycle)
- amount of retrieval practice, spaced, and interleaved learning to build in (New science for successful learning shows that activities to deliver content are most effective, regardless of the learners' experience with the content if they include spaced repetitions, interleaved concepts, and opportunities for retrieval practice.)
- sequence of training activities (how to build their learning and interleave concepts)
- technology that will be used by the learners and how that technology can be capitalized on to aid the learner and provide self-directed learning and performance support.

Example

Learner needs assessment data collection regarding the patient interaction skills training course for nurse's aides revealed, among other things, that:

- these learners are used to being on the run and are not accustomed to sitting in a classroom for a long time
- the training courses will be offered during the last two hours of their shifts
- these learners, although uncomfortable with being in front of a group, have conversations with their peers and their patients most of the day
- they know very little about handling conflict and complaints
- they are experienced at handling interruption; they just choose not to do it well because it causes more stress for them.

Based on this information, the training design of the patient interaction skills training course might include the following activities:

- high-energy levels in the facilitator and in activities to mimic the workplace (learners need to discuss problems and practice with one another)
- role plays beginning with the instructor enacting a role play with learners providing critiques and ending with small group role plays in trios, thereby building intensity and comfort level with the role-play activities
- content presentation followed by structured activities for the "handling complaints" portion
- "discovery" learning for the "handling interruptions" portion

- a nontraining recommendation that nurse's aides' co-workers be trained or provided incentives to avoid piling more interruptions on those nurse's aides who handle interruptions well (nontraining recommendations are discussed in chapter 7).

Getting It Done

To choose the best data collection methods for your needs, you must:

- Know which data you need and how essential it is.
- Analyze the potential methods for feasibility.
- Assess your own skill at implementing each method.
- Understand what parts of your ultimate training design will require data to complete.
- Understand the client's needs, budget, and timeline.

To assess your own level of skill in regard to applying some of the data collection techniques discussed, go back to Table 5-2 and fill in your self-ratings in the column marked "Needs Assessor's Skill Level." Now you can use the complete matrix to assist with making data collection method decisions in your own practice.

Next, take a look at Exercise 5-1 to see how Chris is progressing with the needs assessment project at Whitewater Outfitters.

Exercise 5-1. The Whitewater Outfitter Case Study: Part 4

Chris's challenge was to decide which methods will provide the most useful data and which methods will provide data at multiple needs assessment stages. Using the information contained in this chapter, Chris identified the data collection method(s) that would serve these purposes.

The methods Chris chose are listed in Table 5-3. Compare the list you generated at the end of Exercise 4-1 to Chris's. If you identified most of the same responses as Chris, congratulations! If you missed a few, go back to part 3 of the case and work your way through Chris's list of potential data collection methods, and analyze how he decided which final data collection implementation choices to list in the rightmost column of the data collection plan. Note how Chris selected specific data collection methods for the specific needs identified and did not include all data needs in all methods chosen.

Chris then presented the final list to Emerson for approval. Emerson approved the list, and sent emails to the appropriate individuals to prepare the way for Chris's contact with them. Now, all Chris has to do is implement the data collection process. What tips and warnings would you offer to help Chris implement the data collection efficiently and effectively? List your responses.

Table 5-3. Data Collection Plan

Data Collection Plan				
Project: Interviewing Skills for Team Leaders, Davidson City Plant, Whitewater Outfitters				
Needs Assessment Stage	**Questions to Be Answered**	**Data Source**	**Potential Data Collection Method(s)**	**Data Collection Method**
Stage 1: Business Needs	a. What are the expected revenues for the City Slicker line? b. How much of the expected revenues is the interview skills training for team leaders expected to affect? c. How much of the current turnover can be attributed to the team leaders' current interviewing skills? d. How much of the retail store and customer complaints can be attributed to poor-quality products created by employees who are not good matches for their jobs because of poor hiring decisions and interviewing skills on the part of the team leaders? e. How many of the four EEO complaints in the current fiscal year are due to illegal interview questions? f. How do strong interview skills affect the business? How do they change or support the culture, company vision, and future of the work at the organization?	a. Emerson Stewart, client b. Emerson Stewart, client c. Tracy Waddell, HR, and HR extant data (e.g., turnover data, exit interviews, industry data) d. Riley Johnson, Complaint Center, Syd Diaz and Morgan Ciscyk, other team leaders e. Tracy Waddell, HR, and HR extant data f. Tracy Waddell, HR, and HR extant data	a. Interview Stewart b. Interview Stewart c. Interview Waddell; analysis of extant data d. Interview Johnson; analysis of extant data; interview Diaz and Cisyk; interview team leaders; survey team leaders; focus group of team leaders e. Interview Waddell; analysis of extant data; survey of recent employee hires; survey of former employees f. Interview Waddell; analysis of extant data	a. Interview Stewart b. Interview Stewart c. Interview Waddell; analyze turnover data, industry data, exit interview data d. Interview Johnson; interview Johnson; small group interview of team leaders, including Diaz and Ciscyk; focus group of team leaders e. Interview Waddell; analyze EEO report f. Interview Waddell; analyze interview and hiring data

Table 5-3. Data Collection Plan (continued)

Needs Assessment Stage	Questions to Be Answered	Data Source	Potential Data Collection Method(s)	Data Collection Method
Stage 2: Performance Needs	a. What is the required performance for effective interviewing? b. What does that performance look like? c. How do the team leaders currently conduct interviews? d. What is the team leaders' job environment like?	a. Tracy Waddell, HR b. Other "expert" HR staff, external HR resources (e.g., books, off-the-shelf training, other experts) c. Syd Diaz and Morgan Ciscyk, other team leaders, current team members who have been hired in the last year d. Syd Diaz and Morgan Ciscyk, other team leaders	a. Interview Waddell b. Interview experts and resources; research resources c. Interview Diaz and Ciscyk; observe Diaz and Ciscyk; interview team leaders; focus group of team leaders; observe team leaders; survey recent new hires; interview recent new hires; analyze exit interview data (e.g., HR extant data) d. Interview Diaz and Ciscyk; observe Diaz and Ciscyk; interview team leaders; focus group of team leaders; observe team leaders	a. Interview Waddell b. Purchase external module c. Interview Diaz and Ciscyk; observe Diaz (one-way mirror); focus group of team leaders; analysis of exit interview data d. Observe Diaz (one-way mirror); interview Diaz and Ciscyk; focus group with team leaders

	Questions	Sources	Methods	Data Collection Implementation
Stage 3: Learning Needs	a. What is the skills gap between team leaders' current performance and ideal performance? b. What skills and knowledge must the team leaders learn?	a. Expert HR staff, external HR resources (e.g., books, off-the-shelf training, other experts) b. Expert HR staff, external HR resources (e.g., books, off-the-shelf training, other experts)	a. Interviews, research b. Interviews, research	a. Interview expert HR staff member; small group interview with team leaders b. Purchased module; interview with expert HR staff member
Stage 4: Learner Needs	a. What are the team leaders' backgrounds in interviewing skills? b. What learning activities aid the materials best? How can the activities be presented so they're implemented on the job? c. How do the team leaders feel about the value that interviewing skills bring to this corporate strategy and hiring push?	a. Syd Diaz and Morgan Ciscyk, other team leaders b. Syd Diaz and Morgan Ciscyk, other team leaders, former instructors, extant data from former training evaluations c. Syd Diaz and Morgan Ciscyk, other team leaders	a. Interview Diaz and Ciscyk; observe Diaz and Ciscyk; interview team leaders; focus group of team leaders; observe team leaders b. Interview Diaz and Ciscyk; interview team leaders; focus group of team leaders; observe team leaders; analyze past training evaluation data c. Interview Diaz and Ciscyk; interview team leaders; focus group of team leaders; observe team leaders	a. Focus group with team leaders b. Focus group with team leaders; analysis of past training data (extant)

All right, you have finally implemented your data collection and you have collected your data—now what do you do with it? You'll determine what it all means in chapter 6.

6

Data Analysis

What's Inside This Chapter

This chapter discusses what you discover—what the data tell you about the training need being investigated.
You'll learn:

- the difference between data analysis and recommendations
- the types of data that are identified for each needs assessment stage
- basic information about the role of statistical analysis in training needs assessment
- discussion of nontraining needs assessment results.

6

Data Analysis

Data Analysis Versus Recommendations

Once you have gathered all your needs assessment data, it is time to extract some meaning from the data. As there are separate thought processes in data collection planning, so there are in data analysis as well. Data analysis (step 4 in the needs assessment process) consists of two thought processes that must be kept distinct:

- identifying the key data
- developing recommendations based on the data (Figure 6-1).

What's the difference? To some needs assessors, there isn't much difference, and that's what gets them into trouble. Say, for example, that a needs assessment study focuses on helping a client reduce turnover. Some of the data analysis shows that a large majority (80 percent) of employees who have left the organization in the past year cite job stress as their main reason for leaving. Without putting some intellectual distance between these data and developing a related recommendation, it is very easy to jump to a recommendation that the current employees should undergo stress management training or that their jobs be redesigned to be less stressful. These two potential recommendations are not necessarily supported by the data, but it's easy to make the mistake of thinking that they are.

The data are pure; they are unaffected by the context of the organization or the needs assessor's biases. Simply put, data analysis shows us the *facts* indicated by the data. It presents a clear picture of what is going on in the organization. In this example, the analysis shows that 80 percent of recent former employees said a certain thing. The data don't identify why the former employees said it, the data don't indicate whether what they said is true, and the data certainly don't indicate what should be done about it. The needs assessor will find out these things as the data analysis continues—and when the time comes to identify recommendations.

Figure 6-1. The Training Needs Assessment Process With Step 4 Highlighted

Step 1. Conduct an External and Organization Scan

Step 2. Collect Data to Identify Business Needs

Capitalize on an opportunity
Resolve a problem
Support a strategy

Step 3. Collect Data to Identify Performance, Learning, and Learner Needs

Required performance
Learners' current performance
Required skills and knowledge
Learners' current skills and knowledge
Learner needs

Step 4. Analyze Data

Identify key data: gaps in performance,
skills, and knowledge
Identify recommendations

Step 5. Identify Potential Training Solution

Needed job aids and performance support materials
Types of training methods
Types of training delivery

Step 6. Deliver Data Analysis Feedback

Training recommendations: design and
delivery; ROI or ROE forecast
Nontraining recommendations: work
environment, rewards, consequences,
work processes

Transition Step: Begin Training Design

Recommendations (discussed in chapter 7) are contextual within the organization and situation, as well as with other data. The data analysis provides information about many different organizational aspects in addition to the training needs. Recommendations, rather than being pure, are affected by the

Basic Rule 17

Don't jump from data analysis to a recommendation. Keep these thought processes separate.

needs assessor's job role, areas of responsibility, and client request. In the example regarding former employees' view of benefits, both recommendations are not only flawed, but also outside the purview of a training professional's role. Does that mean nontraining data are not addressed at all in recommendations? No, it means that needs assessment recommendations are carefully crafted based on a number of factors.

Needs assessment data analysis adds value in two ways: by first developing a current picture of what's going on and then by translating the data into action items or recommendations. In fact, this two-part process also provides the framework for how the data analysis and recommendations will be shared with the client when you present your report to your client (discussed in chapter 8).

What Do the Data Say?

The first task in data analysis is to classify and summarize your key data. If your data collection methods were both quantitative and qualitative, you will have both kinds of data to analyze. Quantitative data are usually depicted numerically as frequencies, percentages, or other measures of proportion, as in how many survey respondents said X or Y. Analyzing these data involves determining what the numbers really mean. If 80 percent of survey respondents said X, and 20 percent said Y, what does that mean? This should be clearly separated from what should be done about it. Just like when we separated the data needed from the source of the data back in chapter 3, here we have to be very careful to separate the data analysis from the training recommendation, which we'll develop in chapter 7.

Qualitative data are usually narrative, taking the form of anecdotes, stories, and survey essay questions. Analyzing these kinds of data involves identifying themes, patterns, trends, key ideas, and issues, and determining their strength by examining how often those patterns or trends occur. There may even be opportunities to combine qualitative and quantitative data analysis to determine stronger and more robust patterns and themes. For example, how many employees said

X or *Y* on the survey and how many said the same thing during focus groups? Do the proportions match? What key words from the survey were repeated in the focus group? What key words were not repeated?

Data analysis provides key information for all four needs assessment stages. The following sections describe the kinds of data to expect from your needs assessments.

Stage 1: Business Needs and the Training Initiative

These data relate to:

- importance of the business goal in the client's overall business plan
- strength and clarity of the relationship between business issues and the proposed training solution
- indicators for how much of the business goals the training plan should be expected to achieve
- accuracy of the business indicators in the client's original presenting problem
- additional business indicators that figure into the situation.

Very rarely, if ever, will a training course alone achieve a change in a business indicator; too many other factors in the environment could also have an effect on the business indicator. For example, say a company introduces a new product and the organization's expectation is that over-all company sales will increase by 20 percent in the second quarter after the product is introduced and the new product sales training has taken place. There are many organizational and market-place factors—including marketing, advertising, customer demand, and other efforts—that can affect the sales of this new product; the new product sales training is only one factor.

The training professional and client should negotiate what proportion of that 20 percent increase the training alone should be expected to achieve and how they will know that the train-ing was helpful. This can be the beginning of the evaluation and measurement that will be needed later on after the training is implemented (see *Evaluation Basics*, 2nd edition, for further details on developing an evaluation plan). Partner with the client to develop the business expec-tations. When you can document this and achieve it, you will further earn credibility with your business partners.

Stage 2: Specific Desired Work Performance

These data relate to:

- results expected from job performers

- how job performers should achieve those results; performance standards
- background information regarding the job environment, tools, and processes used when employees perform the targeted skills
- organizational factors (nontraining factors) other than knowledge or skill deficiencies that affect performance
- indicators regarding transfer strategies that might be required in the training design.

Identifying job performance standards for employees who will be in the proposed training is important because this information will be translated into measurement tools during the training course. Some performance standards focus on the *process* of task accomplishment. The assumption is that if a performer accomplishes the task steps in a prescribed way, the task will be done perfectly. Other performance standards focus on the task *product*. In this case, the assumption is that it doesn't matter what steps the performer takes—what matters is that the product produced meets specific quality standards. If it does, then the task will have been done perfectly.

Stage 3: Training Design Information

These data relate to:

- learning objectives
- indicators for learning activities that will replicate the job environment
- background information to replicate the job environment for skill practices
- test items for knowledge assessments
- process and product checklists for skill practice assessments
- how learners value (or not) the skills to be taught
- other attitudinal information about the learners.

Identifying learner attitudes and how they value the skills to be taught is important. As discussed in chapter 5, you're likely to encounter occasions when the training design must include buy-in for learning activities to persuade and influence the learners in their attitudes toward the skills and the learning.

Stage 4: Training Delivery Information

These data relate to:

- physical environment indicators
- training delivery methods
- facilitation and delivery process standards.

The physical learning environment plays a big part in helping learners learn. If the environment is not a conducive one, the learners will be distracted, which creates barriers to learning. Needs assessment data analysis will provide information regarding optimal physical aspects of the learning environment. Examples include size, layout, furniture setup and placement, space required for movement or activities, groupings of learners, technological equipment (projectors, television, and so forth), and amenities (refreshments and handouts) required.

There are a number of types of training delivery methods that are useful to build skills and knowledge. The best methods to use are those that closely mimic the environment in which they will be used. For example, if the skill to be developed is conversational, this is usually best done in person with peers and a facilitator. If the learners need knowledge on a product or need to be able to look up schematics about a product, then an online course where they get to practice this may be necessary. There are many different training delivery methods—blended learning (a blend of online, self-study, and facilitated training), flipped learning (where learners read the "lecture" materials at home and then go to a facilitated training session to practice using the material and receive feedback), traditional instructor-led training, online instructor-led training, online web-based (self-study) training, mobile learning, and social learning, to name a few.

If the training needs to be delivered by a live facilitator, then facilitation process standards are needed. These are standards for how a training course is to be facilitated and guide how the facilitator will teach the training course. Some process standards are generated by the subject matter, the training designer, and the facilitator. Examples include:

- encouraging questions
- directing learner questions back to the learners to give them "first crack"
- debriefing an activity to focus on application back to the job
- basing facilitation on principles of adult learning
- basing the level of learner materials on their backgrounds and experience
- emphasizing different content segments based on learners' needs
- basing instructional strategy on content and how it will be used
- grouping learners based on organizational levels of learners and the implications of information that might be shared during the training.

Other facilitation process standards are generated by information about the learners gleaned in the needs assessment. Examples of learner information and corresponding process standards are provided in Table 6-1. Similar standards need to be developed based on the training delivery method determined.

Table 6-1. Examples of Facilitation Process Standards Based on Learner Information

Learner Information	Process Standards
Learners are not used to sitting still; their jobs are physically active.	Learning activities must include physical movement that will replicate the job environment.
Learners are apprehensive about using the skill set in the training; their confidence level is not very high.	Incorporate several activities that focus on "What barriers make this hard?" and "How can we overcome the barriers?" Break learning segments into small segments so that learners experience incremental successes.

A Short Side Trip to Descriptive Statistical Analysis

It is rare for training professionals to enter the field because of their excitement about conducting statistical analysis during the needs assessment process. Nevertheless, there are times when a statistical analysis of a quantitative set of data (usually found in extant data, test scores, survey responses, and the like) is very

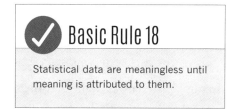

Basic Rule 18

Statistical data are meaningless until meaning is attributed to them.

useful. Statistical data analysis provides key data and evidence that will drive your recommendations. However, you must attribute meaning to the data; they are meaningless until you do that.

Descriptive Statistics

The way you attribute meaning to statistical data is through the use of descriptive statistics. Descriptive statistics are methods of interpreting data that enable meaning to be derived. There may be times that you are actually conducting statistical analysis and must determine what the statistics mean. On other occasions you may see a reference to statistical analysis in extant data that you have gathered or in a journal article you have read. A basic understanding of descriptive statistics is useful to help you perform your own calculations to guide you in being an intelligent consumer of statistical analysis. Following are descriptions of basic descriptive statistical methods:

- **Interval scale:** A scale in which the difference between two values measured on the scale has the same meaning. This implies that scores may meaningfully be added or subtracted. (Example: Test scores on a scale of 0 to 100.) Interval scales can also be used in an answer scale on a survey or questionnaire in which the meanings of the various scale levels are defined to be at equal intervals. (Example: A survey in which the answers are on a 4-point scale: 1 = strongly disagree; 2 = disagree; 3 = agree; 4 = strongly agree.) In this case, the intervals between the scale items are defined to be equal.

- **Nominal scale:** A type of scale with a limited number of possible outcomes that cannot be placed in any order representing their relative value. (Examples: female versus male; age groups.)
- **Reliability:** The extent to which a test or measuring procedure yields the same results on repeated trials.
- **Validity:** The extent to which a test or measuring procedure measures what it is purported to measure.
- **Frequency:** The number of times a value appears in a data set.
- **Mean:** The value that is computed by dividing the sum of a set of terms by the number of terms; also called the average.
- **Median:** The value in an ordered set of values below and above which there is an equal number of values.
- **Mode:** The most frequent value of a set of data.
- **Percentile:** A descriptive scale that demonstrates how a score or measure compares with other measures in the same data set. For example, in a set of test scores, if a specific score is at the 80th percentile, 20 percent of the test scores in the set are greater than this score and 80 percent of the test scores are less than this score (regardless of the actual numerical value of the test score itself).
- **Significance:** A test for determining the probability (p) that a given result did not occur just by chance. For example, if the data derived from a set of test scores are "significant at the $p = 0.01$ level," it means that there is a 1 percent possibility that the test results occurred by chance and a 99 percent possibility that the test results demonstrate a pattern. A p value greater than 0.10 (10 percent possibility that the test results occurred purely by chance) is generally considered to be low significance.

 Basic Rule 19

In statistics, the significance of the data is not the same as the importance of the data. The term refers to statistical significance—the probability (p) that the results occurred purely by chance.

Inferential Statistics

Another set of statistics is called inferential statistics. Rather than describing the data as in descriptive statistics, inferential statistics are used to present various relationships among values in the data set. Conclusions about the data can then be inferred from an examination of the statistics.

The most common inferential statistic that you are probably familiar with is standard deviation, which is a measure of how much variability exists in the data set. If the data points are widely scattered or if the data set is small, the standard deviation is going to be greater than if the data points are close together or if the data set is large.

Further exploration of statistical analysis, both descriptive and inferential, is beyond the scope of this book. Several references in the Additional Resources section can provide more detail regarding statistical analysis of needs assessment data.

Using Statistics to Derive Meaning

You've heard the expression, "Statistics don't lie; statisticians do." That's a very cynical way of saying that statistical results can be presented and interpreted in more than one way to achieve different goals. This point will come into play in chapter 8, in which delivering feedback to the client is discussed. However, it also fits well into the context of this discussion. Consider the following example:

- Exit interview data from employees who have left the organization in the past year were analyzed.
- The number of former employees represented in the data was 40.
- Of these 40 former employees, 18 (45 percent of total respondents) said that "low salary" was a major reason for their leaving.
- Out of those 18, 10 said that "lack of training and development opportunities" was a second major reason for leaving (56 percent of the 18; 25 percent of total respondents).

Could it be said that "almost half" of the former employees cited low salary? Yes, if you want to highlight a salary issue. Could it be said that "less than half" of the former employees cited low salary? Yes, if you want to downplay the salary issue. Could it be said that "more than half," or 56 percent, of those who cited low salary also cited lack of training and development opportunities? Yes, if you want to highlight the training and development issue. Could it be said that "only 25 percent" of the total respondents cited the lack of training and development opportunities? Yes, if you want to downplay the training and development issue.

Is each of these results correct and true? Yes. Is each intended to influence the client in a different direction? Yes. Is it ethical to present data in this manner? You make the call. There is a fine line between influence and manipulation in the world of statistical analysis. Where that line is depends on the situation, the client, and the inherent risk for the training professional in making flawed data interpretations. Here are two suggestions:

- When you have statistical analysis that provides indicators that aren't very strong, seek additional corroborating data from your other sources and methods to bolster or refute the statistical analysis.
- If it doesn't feel right, it probably isn't.

Gather all your data, and then use the numbers that correlate and support each other and also pertain to your business needs. But be on the lookout for data that "don't fit." These data could be trying to tell you something important. Review these atypical data with your client to gain further insight into how or if they fit.

Your short side trip to descriptive statistical analysis is now complete. It was mentioned earlier that a presentation of the complexity of more than basic statistics is beyond the scope of this book. You are encouraged to educate yourself so that you can understand basic statistical analysis and be a good "statistics consumer." Beyond that, if your needs assessment study truly requires the rigor of more advanced statistical analysis, it is recommended that you hire a statistician or see if there is a statistician or data analyst available at the organization.

Nontraining Needs

Do you remember the scenario presented in chapter 2 about how clients request training and how tempting it is to simply say "Yes, what time?" When that scenario is played out, the so-called needs assessment (if any takes place at all) is focused on the training only: What should the schedule be? How many lessons? What learning activities to include? Because a true training needs assessment focuses on job performance and how training can support it, it places the training in the big picture of how it will support the business. And, because data collection and analysis in this case are broader in scope, one inevitable (and highly desired) result is the identification of nontraining-related items as well as training-related items.

Why is the identification of nontraining issues a desired outcome? Whether the focus is on a business problem, opportunity, or strategy, training itself only supports job performance that is related to knowledge and skill deficiencies. Lack of job performance (and the ensuing lack of business results) is usually due to multiple factors, only some of which are related to training.

Think About This

Being able to identify nontraining issues as barriers to performance is the key to making the leap from training to human performance improvement (HPI). "HPI is . . . a systemic and systematic approach to identifying the barriers that prevent people from achieving top performance. . . . If people are to achieve top-level performance, [you must] optimize all the components of their human performance system. With each barrier in the system, their performance decreases" (Fuller 1999). The job of the human performance consultant is to remove as many of the barriers as possible or practical through any variety of initiatives, including training.

Clients sometimes make the assumption that training is the only answer. If you allow that assumption to continue, sooner or later results will occur that don't meet the business needs. The client will return to you, saying "My business need wasn't met! Your training didn't work!" Your credibility could be damaged or lost entirely in the eyes of this client. Just as you can't isolate training as the reason for all positive results, you can't isolate training as the reason for all negative results or lack of results.

Instead, negotiate (as much as possible) a proper needs assessment with the client in the beginning because a proper needs assessment focuses on the big picture of job performance and its impact on the business. In doing so, your guiding question is: "If the training itself is an overwhelming success, what else is going on that could prevent improved job performance and thus prevent the attainment of business needs?"

Examples of nontraining issues that affect job performance include:

- **tools:** lack of equipment, not enough for all to use, obsolete equipment
- **regulations:** organizational or governmental regulations that prevent people from performing in the way required to achieve business results
- **organizational structure:** structure that is too narrowly or broadly defined to allow for required accountabilities and performance
- **customers:** changes in customer needs and interests that affect business results
- **external pressures:** competition, market influences, time of year, weather, political environment, current events
- **workforce:** demographics, number of people with desired skill sets, cultural differences, age or generational differences, seasoned versus new employees
- **resources:** equipment, facilities, people, time, money, work processes, and organizational policies that support desired behaviors

- **incentives:** rewards for desired performance are not matched to performance, or worse, there are no rewards for performance; conversely, rewards inadvertently given for lack of performance, or the wrong behavior is rewarded
- **on-the-job reinforcement:** lack of practice opportunities, no reward for incremental successes, little or no managerial support or feedback
- **organizational culture:** nonsupportive culture including work and time pressures, contradictory organizational values, insufficient authority
- **motivation:** lack of desire to perform (although not lack of skill).

As you can see, there are many potential nontraining influences on job performance and, ultimately, organizational needs. Because you identify them in the data analysis step, should you make recommendations regarding them as part of the needs assessment process? That question is addressed in chapter 7.

Getting It Done

Data analysis is literally what the data mean—the facts and indicators that the data signify to you, the client, business partners, and stakeholders regarding what is going on in the organization about a potential training need. It is important to represent the analysis in a way that is as unvarnished and unembellished as possible, so meaning can be determined.

Exercise 6-1 presents a data set for you to practice calculating the frequency, mean, median, and mode. The answers immediately follow the exercise.

Exercise 6-1. Descriptive Statistics Practice

A knowledge test with 100 items was administered to 20 participants. The possible score range for the test was 0 (no correct answers) to 100 (all correct answers). Following are the test scores:

Person A	Person B	Person C	Person D	Person E	Person F	Person G	Person H	Person I	Person J
Score: 98	Score: 100	Score: 87	Score: 63	Score: 60	Score: 79	Score: 87	Score: 52	Score: 84	Score: 91
Person K	Person L	Person M	Person N	Person O	Person P	Person Q	Person R	Person S	Person T
Score: 98	Score: 89	Score: 87	Score: 72	Score: 75	Score: 59	Score: 68	Score: 93	Score: 80	Score: 68

1. What is the frequency distribution for these test scores?

2. What is the mean of these scores?

3. What is the median of these scores?

4. What is the mode of these scores?

Answers

1. The frequency distribution for the test scores is:

Score	Frequency		Score	Frequency
100	1		79	1
98	2		75	1
93	1		72	1
91	1		68	2
89	1		63	1
87	3		60	1
84	1		59	1
80	1		52	1

2. The mean for these scores is the sum of the scores divided by the number of scores: 1,590 ÷ 20 = 79.5.

3. The median for these scores is the value(s) below and above which there is an equal number of values.
   100, 98, 98, 93, 91, 89, 87, 87, 87, **84, 80**, 79, 75, 72, 68, 68, 63, 60, 59, 52
   (There is a double median, which can occur.)

4. The mode for these scores is the most frequently occurring value: 87.
   (When multiple values occur with the same frequency, the distribution is bimodal, trimodal, or multimodal.)

Chris did a good job in identifying the things to watch out for as the data collection implementation began. Now, what do the data show (Exercise 6-2)?

Exercise 6-2. Whitewater Outfitters Case Study: Part 5

Before beginning the data collection implementation, Chris carefully thought through the process to plan for contingencies:

- Be careful not to "contradict" Emerson in the next interview by mentioning hunches.
- Ask Waddell and Johnson what indicators for job interviewing *they* think the extant data they are supplying show.
- Conduct the joint interview with Diaz and Ciscyk *before* the team leader focus group, to get information to shape focus group questions.
- Ask another training or HR person to assist with conducting the focus group and interpreting focus group results.
- Structure some focus group questions to check out the results of the joint interview with Diaz and Ciscyk.
- Interview Diaz after observation to get at the thoughts that drive interview behaviors.
- Ask someone internal who has a statistical background to help analyze extant data.
- Email a progress report to Emerson every few days to report what was done, a few of the most interesting findings, and what will be implemented next.
- Keep track of Emerson's reactions to the progress reports (items that caught interest, ways of expression that were confusing to Emerson, questions Emerson asked in response). These items could be indicators for structuring the needs assessment report to Emerson later.

Compare your list of tips and warnings from Exercise 5-1 with Chris's list. If you identified most of the same responses as Chris, congratulations! If you identified even more than Chris, way to go! If you missed a few, go back to the case descriptions in earlier chapters and see if you can spot the indicators for Chris's list.

Chris then analyzed the data to identify results. Table 6-2 lists Chris's results without going into the actual data analysis.

Now your work begins:

1. In the third column, place a check mark next to the results that Emerson (the client) was correct about.

2. In the fourth column, indicate with an arrow (→) each finding that represents new information that had not been identified by Emerson.

3. In the fifth column, place a *T* next to each finding that is training related and *NT* next to each finding that is not training related.

4. In the sixth column, jot down the data source that provided each finding.

5. Now, answer this question: Given these results, what should Chris recommend to Emerson? List your recommendations here.

Table 6-2. Data Analysis

Needs Assessment Stage	Data Analysis	Was Emerson Right (✓)?	Was Information New to Emerson (→)?	Training (T) or Nontraining (NT)?	Data Source
Stage 1: Business Needs	The upcoming hiring push will require the team leaders to have interviewing skills.				
	Two of the four EEO complaints in the past fiscal year relate directly to team leaders having asked illegal interview questions.				
	A glitch in the shipping process caused 85 percent of customer and retail store complaints in the past six months. Shipping is not part of the production process.				
	Turnover is higher than the industry average. There is a direct connection between the higher turnover and the following four factors: • Team leaders are making poor hiring decisions, resulting in turnover due to stress and burnout (in underqualified new hires) and boredom (in overqualified new hires). • A common source of stress for all team members occurs during midday hours when fellow team members take lunch breaks and the same amount of work must be done with fewer people on the line. • Team members are stressed by the large amount of negative and critical feedback they receive from their team leaders regarding the perceived production problems (and team leaders are getting the same negative and critical feedback themselves). • There is a common perception among employees that Eddie Bean's benefits are better than Whitewater Outfitter's benefits.				

Table 6-2. Data Analysis (continued)

Needs Assessment Stage	Data Analysis	Was Emerson Right (✓)?	Was Information New to Emerson (→)?	Training (T) or Nontraining (NT)?	Data Source
Stage 2: Performance Needs	Interview techniques are inconsistent among team leaders and vary from candidate to candidate. Team leaders need to conduct interviews that are consistent from team leader to team leader and from candidate to candidate.				
	Little or no preparation is done for interviews, so team leaders will need to learn how to prepare for interviews.				
	Team leaders currently just ramble and chat during interviews, so they will need to learn how to structure interviews.				
	Interview questions are not well designed; they are obvious and leading. Team leaders need to ask well-designed interview questions so they can accurately assess candidates' potential fit for production jobs.				
	Team leaders are not familiar with and do not use legal, job-related interview questions. They need to start using them.				
	Current hiring decisions result in mismatched hires at least 50 percent of the time. Team leaders need to use objective, consistent criteria to make well-matched hiring decisions.				
Stage 3: Learning Needs	At the end of the training session, learners must be able to do the following: • Prepare for an interview. • Analyze applications and resumes. • Develop focused, job-related interview questions. • Ask legal interview questions. • Conduct an interview. • Make a hiring decision using objective criteria.				

Stage 4: Learner Needs	The learners work mostly in teams with their own team or in a team of team leaders; they are not used to working alone.				
	The fast-paced, stressful environment allows little time to stay focused on one task.				
	The learners know that they need the training.				
	The learners are fearful of not doing well in training and being embarrassed.				
	The learners are not used to sitting in a classroom; they usually move around on the job.				

Data analysis is the "what" of needs assessment—what is going on. Recommendations are the "how" of needs assessment—how the data will be used to shape the potential training initiative and other influences so that business and performance needs can be achieved. Chapter 7 focuses on recommendations.

7

Data Analysis Recommendations

 What's Inside This Chapter

This chapter demonstrates the difference between data and recommendations. You'll learn:

- why it's important to separate the processes of identifying data analysis findings and data analysis recommendations
- how to develop training recommendations
- how to develop nontraining recommendations
- how to make an ROI forecast.

7

Data Analysis Recommendations

Recommendations Are Not the Same as Data Analysis

The first purpose of a training needs assessment study is to determine how a training initiative must affect job performance to meet business needs (training needs). The second purpose is to identify what else must change in the organization to support the desired performance (nontraining needs). Both of these purposes should be addressed in the training needs assessment recommendations. Chapter 6 addressed both training and nontraining data. This chapter continues with step 5 of the needs assessment process: the development of training and nontraining recommendations (see Figure 7-1).

Again, it is critical to separate the two thought processes of identifying key data and developing recommendations. You'll recall that data collection planning entails three separate thought processes, and the purpose of keeping them separate is to avoid prematurely narrowing down potential choices.

By the same token, data analysis and recommendations are separated into two thought processes to avoid the same premature narrowing-down effect. The danger here is that key data can have a recommendation embedded within it, making it easy and tempting to jump to that recommendation. For example, "Many employees believe the benefits program is not as good as other employers' programs" has a potential recommendation embedded within it: "Improve the company's benefits program." But this is too easy. While it could be correct, many times it is not. These key data have to be compared with other data, patterns and trends must be identified, and the context within which the data were gathered must be analyzed.

 **Basic Rule 20**

Keep the thought process of identifying analysis separate from the thought process of developing recommendations.

Figure 7-1. The Training Needs Assessment Process With Step 5 Highlighted

Step 1. Conduct an External and Organization Scan

Step 2. Collect Data to Identify Business Needs

Capitalize on an opportunity
Resolve a problem
Support a strategy

Step 3. Collect Data to Identify Performance, Learning, and Learner Needs

Required performance
Learners' current performance
Required skills and knowledge
Learners' current skills and knowledge
Learner needs

Step 4. Analyze Data

Identify key data: gaps in performance,
skills, and knowledge
Identify recommendations

Step 5. Identify Potential Training Solution

Needed job aids and performance support materials
Types of training methods
Types of training delivery

Step 6. Deliver Data Analysis Feedback

Training recommendations: design and
delivery; ROI or ROE forecast
Nontraining recommendations: work
environment, rewards, consequences,
work processes

Transition Step: Begin Training Design

Making Training Recommendations

Training recommendations are just that: recommendations that the training professional develops to meet the training-related needs that were identified in the needs assessment study. Training recommendations usually include:

- learning objectives for the to-be-developed training course
- parts of the training course content that should be emphasized or de-emphasized to maximize the business impact
- activities to focus on particular skills; because of the needs identified for a particular course or audience, you may recommend that some content be addressed simply at the knowledge level, whereas other content that is more important for the business goals should be addressed more deeply and taken to the level of skill practice
- types of learning activities and training materials (such as visuals, verbal content, references, handouts, notebooks, manuals, and so forth)
- delivery methods (including self-study, classroom, classroom and lab, small group, distance learning, mobile learning, or combinations thereof)
- type of learning environment, pre-work, post-work, prerequisites, training schedule
- audience (type of learners the recommended training is best suited for depending on their organizational levels, background, experience, and expertise).

 Think About This

The nature of training recommendations provides another example of how closely a training needs assessment is related to training design, and how the line between them can become blurred. The entire practice of implementing training—start to finish—is an iterative and interdependent process.

Making Nontraining Recommendations

Is it the training professional's role to identify nontraining issues and make nontraining recommendations? Unequivocally, yes. When identifying key data, it is appropriate and necessary for the training professional to ask, "What else is going on in the organization that, even if the training program is an unparalleled success, might prevent the attainment of performance and business goals?" It is, therefore, appropriate and necessary for the training professional to develop recommendations to mitigate these nontraining issues based on the data that were collected.

There are several reasons why you should do this:

- Because all the factors affecting job performance are addressed, this comprehensive approach promises the highest likelihood that job performance goals (and, therefore, business goals) will be achieved.

 Basic Rule 21

Training recommendations involve all aspects of the proposed training effort.

- The training effort has the best chance of succeeding in its goals because other contributing factors are also addressed.
- You are focusing on the big picture of job performance, not just meeting a training need.
- You are seen not just as a training provider but as a collaborative consultant and partner who enjoys credibility with the client (see chapter 2).
- You can build skills as a performance consultant.
- Developing nontraining recommendations in addition to training recommendations supports the survival of the training function (see chapter 2). If the client chooses not to address nontraining recommendations, and subsequently the business and performance needs goals are not met, the training effort does not become the scapegoat for the failure. In a worst-case scenario, you have documentation that you identified other factors that were involved and should have been addressed.

 Basic Rule 22

It is appropriate and necessary to develop both training and nontraining recommendations resulting from a needs assessment study.

When key data are identified, the information gleaned is simply that—information. Making recommendations involves deciding what should be done with that information. When the data are training-related, identifying a recommendation is your job. For example, if the data show that "The learner audience's jobs are fast-paced and highly stressful," a training professional would know that the training design must replicate the job environment as much as possible to support transfer. Thus, the corresponding recommendation might be to "design learning activities that are fast-paced and create manageable levels of stress." With nontraining-related data, however, there are more challenges. The nontraining issue is not necessarily an area of expertise for the training professional, and others may think that making nontraining recommendations is not part of the training professional's role.

How to structure nontraining recommendations is also a function of the scope, level, and assigned area of the needs assessor's job role and areas of responsibility. Nontraining recommendations are also subject to other contextual factors, such as the relationship among the training and nontraining data that were identified, the client's amount of understanding and willingness to tackle the big picture of performance, and the organizational culture.

Challenging as it may be, it is not only appropriate to make nontraining recommendations, but it is also an essential part of your job. Remember, your goal is to go from training order taker to training consultant to performance consultant. This is critical to your credibility and ability to partner with your clients to uncover the barriers to business performance. But, how do you do it and what do you do?

Do you recall the example in chapter 6? There was nontraining evidence that 80 percent of recent former employees said job stress was the primary reason they left the organization. At the data analysis stage in chapter 6, there was no other information to be gleaned. This information was a fact, and no action could be taken at that time. Now, as you move from the analysis stage into recommendations, you must make recommendations about what should be done about that fact. Remember, the business need in the example was to reduce turnover. Here are some possibilities for nontraining recommendations regarding workplace stress:

- Survey current employees to see if they have job stress. If they do, find out what is causing the stress and see if there is something that can be done to reduce it. If they don't, do nothing.
- Redesign jobs so that they are less stressful.
- Do nothing. After all, only 30 people out of a large employee population said it—and they're already gone.
- Develop a stress management training program.
- Add benefits that help handle stress—such as a gym membership.
- Research other patterns in the data from former employees to see if there are other patterns among the people who reported job stress (for example, inadequate employee orientation or other backgrounds and experiences in common).
- Research job stress in the organization to find out how employees define it and what they think causes it.

- Perform a second training needs assessment, but this time for the stress issue alone. Determine whether training, job restructuring, or other options are needed.

Which answer do you think is best? All of the above? None of the above? It depends? The correct answer is "it depends," and it depends on four factors:

- **How these data relate in context with other training and nontraining data:** There may be other indicators in the data that tell you how critical the job stress evidence is in the context of the entire needs assessment study.
- **The training professional's role and level in the organization:** For example, a training professional who is part of an HR department will most likely choose different recommendations than a training professional who is part of the operations group because of differences in internal perceptions, organizational hierarchy, and politics. Some of the recommendations would be appropriate for an operations training professional to make but not for an HR training professional and vice versa.
- **Perception of the training function within the organization:** If the training function is already seen as an internal consulting function that focuses on job performance, recommendations will be chosen differently and in a broader scope than in an organization in which the training function is perceived as a training provider on request.
- **Cost of implementing a recommendation compared with how much benefit will be derived from it:** This factor relates to the process of forecasting the return on the investment in training or nontraining solutions.

Deciding upon nontraining recommendations and how to position them are very important judgment calls that involve multiple considerations and conversations with the client and other business partners.

So, What About ROI?

Should an ROI forecast be part of the recommendations that come out of a needs assessment study? ROI analysis is usually discussed as a part of the training evaluation process. It is an analysis that is calculated after training is complete, and compares the net benefits of training with the costs of the training. Whether or not to calculate ROI is something that is decided in the needs assessment process. If the project is seen as something very critical to the business, there may be more of an emphasis on the need for the training evaluation to include ROI. This again is determined based on discussions with the client.

The ROI calculation is:

(Net benefits ÷ Costs) x 100 = ROI (%)

An ROI of 100 percent means that the training project paid for itself. An ROI that exceeds 100 percent means that the training project produced a return on the initial investment. For example, an ROI of 200 percent means that the training project returned to the organization twice what it cost; an ROI of 1,000 percent means that the training project returned 10 times its cost to the organization.

ROI actually has its beginnings in the needs assessment process. One of the ways that training professionals "sell" their clients on the potential value of a training project is by forecasting, or projecting, its potential ROI. Being able to forecast a positive ROI can be very persuasive; for some clients, ROI is what convinces them to invest in the project. Following are the steps for establishing an ROI forecast.

 Think About This

The entire practice of implementing training—start to finish—is an iterative and interdependent process. The practice of forecasting ROI or ROE is another example of how closely training needs assessment is related to training evaluation and how the line between them can become blurred.

Step 1

The first step is to calculate the projected value of the business goal. In many cases, the client has already done that for you. For example, an expected increase in sales can easily be translated into a dollar figure; an expected decrease in waste can also be translated into dollars. Other, so-called soft measures (for example, customer satisfaction ratings or turnover rates) can have dollar values attributed to them by the specialists who work with those extant data: The HR department can often tell you what a certain reduction in turnover would save the company. Many marketing departments can tell you what a particular increase in customer satisfaction would make for the organization. For soft measures that have never been calculated, you can use your ingenuity to develop a calculation yourself.

For example, say that you received a training request for a course for first-line supervisors in how to handle grievances. Your client says that there are too many grievances being escalated past the first-line supervisor stage. When high-level managers and executives have to adjudicate grievances, it wastes their time and the company's resources. You could first calculate an average hourly salary for managers and executives. Then, you could calculate how many grievances are escalated past the first-line supervisor level in a set time period (a quarter, a year) and find out the average number of hours it takes to adjudicate a grievance. If you then multiply the hourly salary times the number of grievances times the average number of hours per grievance, you arrive at the current cost of escalated grievances—the business problem that needs to be resolved.

How much reduction in cost does your client want to achieve? There is no magic formula here. With guidance from historical data and the analysis from the current needs assessment study, your client should be able to define a business goal. In this case, how much reduction in cost due to escalated grievances would indicate success to the client? How many fewer escalated grievances does that equal? This discussion results in the identification of the business goal.

Think About This

The Additional Resources section provides more help in calculating dollar amounts for soft measures. Some examples include complaints, customer satisfaction, quality, turnover, absenteeism, and morale.

Step 2

In collaboration with your client, estimate a reasonable proportion of effect that training can be expected to have on the desired business outcome. Building on the previous example, say that X is the current cost of escalated grievances. What percentage of X can you and your client agree on as an expected effect of the grievance training course? Guide your client in think-

Basic Rule 23

Work with your client to isolate the expected effects of training through estimates.

ing about other nontraining data that have been identified as having an effect on the number of escalated grievances (for example, hard-to-understand policies, lack of first-line supervisor desire or motivation to adjudicate grievances, lack of reward for doing it well, or inadvertent "punishment" for choosing not to adjudicate grievances).

There's no magic formula here. Whatever you and your client can agree on as a reasonable estimate is, well, reasonable. In the example, say you and your client reach the conclusion that 20 percent of *X* is a reasonable expectation for the effect of training. This figure is the expected benefit from training.

 Noted

Some people are troubled by the use of estimates in ROI forecasting (in training needs assessment) and calculation (in training evaluation). But every time people attempt to predict the future in business, they are using estimates—whether setting life insurance premiums or identifying weather patterns that will influence crops. Remember, when estimates are made by experts in that aspect of the business (in this case, your client), they become extremely well-educated estimates. When identifying ROI estimates with your client make sure that you and your client both agree that it is a reasonable estimate.

Step 3

Calculate the projected costs of the potential training effort, including needs assessment, design, development, delivery, and evaluation. Here are some costs to consider:

- salaries and benefits of needs assessors, designers, developers, facilitators, and support staff
- salaries and benefits of employees who participate in the needs assessment
- travel and expenses for all
- contractor's fees
- office supplies and equipment
- purchased materials
- photocopying costs for materials
- mailing and shipping costs
- salaries and benefits of the training participants
- media
- artwork, copyrights, royalties
- training facilities.

Step 4

Calculate the projected ROI:

Expected Benefits – Projected Costs = Net Expected Benefits

(Net Expected Benefits ÷ Projected Costs) x 100 = ROI (%)

Step 5

Present the projected ROI as part of your recommendations. Depending on the projected ROI, your client may or may not be sold on the training initiative. There is no magic formula here, either. In some cases, as long as a training plan pays for itself (an ROI of 100 percent), that's good enough. In other cases, the client may require a substantially positive projected ROI to give the "go" order.

This is a critical point. If the client doesn't think the projected ROI is sufficient, then you will need to discuss the ROI and alternatives with them. Is there a problem with the way the ROI was projected or determined? If so, make adjustments and then present the revised ROI to your client. If the projected ROI is calculated correctly, but still provides less of a positive impact than the client expects or needs to approve the cost of the training project, it is time to discuss alternative options for solving the business need. The training needs assessment may show that it costs too much to try to fix the problem, and fixing the problem will only provide a minimal benefit. This is very important information for your clients to know, because they may decide that it's not worth it to fix the problem. If this is their conclusion, then the training project will either be put on hold or cancelled.

If the client still needs some sort of solution to the business problem, but the projected training recommendation costs more to implement than the business will see in positive results, you may be able to find a way to reduce the costs of the training. There also may be nontraining solutions that can be implemented first. Have a discussion with the client regarding which nontraining solution would provide the most positive impact. Determine the projected ROI of the nontraining solutions, and see if they will provide a positive business impact that meets the client's expectations. You may have to hand the project over to another department at this point if the nontraining initiatives are outside the expertise and scope of the training department.

Tips for Projecting ROI

Why project ROI at all? Some clients are very bottom-line oriented, and the language of ROI is very meaningful to them. Being able to project ROI shows that you understand your client's need for a bottom-line impact on business measures. Keep these tips in mind as you start to project ROI for your training projects:

- Level 4 evaluation and ROI are not the same thing. Level 4 involves the business measure itself. In the example, the Level 4 business goal is to reduce the number of escalated grievances by 20 percent. The ROI process simply assigns a monetary value to that business measure (number of grievances) and compares it with the costs. ROI, in fact, is often called Level 5 evaluation (Phillips and Phillips 2016).

- If the forecasted ROI is less than 100 percent, then your training project will cost more than the expected benefit to the organization. For some clients, you may choose not to include the ROI projection for that reason. Other clients will approve such a project anyway and assume any lost resources as opportunity cost. Still others will ask that you find a way to lower the costs to implement the training project to increase the ROI.

- If you choose to forecast ROI, you better achieve it! ROI is a powerful tool for convincing a client that a training project will affect the problem. It can also damage a training professional's credibility if the expected ROI isn't achieved once the course is evaluated. That's why isolating the expected effects of training, and agreeing on them, with your client is important. What is an acceptable ROI to support a go or no-go decision? That is up to your client. Having your clients select the ROI measures and determine the qualifications up front will help them buy into the training solution and pave the way to justify the training plan with other business partners and stakeholders.

- There is no rule about what an acceptable ROI forecast is for a training project. That decision depends on your client and how your client chooses to view the many contextual factors that will affect the ROI.

 Think About This

Some clients are not interested in ROI, especially as far as soft measures are concerned. If the goal is to reduce absenteeism by a certain percentage and that reduction occurs, they don't find it necessary to express that achievement in dollars and cents. This is where ROE may be a more appropriate measure. If your client is satisfied with the outcome as it is, there is no need for you to push for an ROI measurement.

"When you get a new hammer, everything in the world looks like a nail." Remember that expression when you think about ROI. This process has become very popular in the training field and for good reason. It is a very powerful, persuasive tool in needs assessment, and a very powerful tool to demonstrate impact in evaluation. It is not, however, the be-all and end-all. It is a way of quantifying the potential benefit of a training initiative. The potential benefit is still there (for example, reduction in number of escalated grievances); the ROI forecast simply translates that potential benefit into a dollar amount so it can be compared with potential costs.

ROI can only be used when all the other components in the training system are present and support it. If you are not conducting a thorough needs assessment focused on both training and nontraining findings, do not forecast an ROI. Likewise, if you are not conducting evaluation at Levels 1-4, do not calculate ROI during your evaluation (McCain 2015). You will have no interim measures from evaluation Levels 1-4 to serve as indicators for making adjustments along the way.

Or Is It ROE?

What if the client isn't interested in ROI at all? If the needs assessment is new to the client, she may also not be used to calculating ROI. Or maybe the client can't see how training can be isolated enough to quantify and calculate a results and return on investment. Further, maybe the client isn't used to determining a value and just needs to see a change in behavior or the reduction of a specific problem. In these cases, return on expectations (ROE) is another measure that many clients find useful. This was proposed as a measure of evaluation for training programs from James and Wendy Kirkpatrick (2011). In ROE, you discuss with your clients what they expect to see as a result of training. They then determine what their expectations are and you put together recommendations on how those expectations could be achieved through training and nontraining solutions.

Getting It Done

The goal for a needs assessment study is to produce recommendations. A complete set of recommendations focuses on both training and nontraining issues that are affecting the business and performance goals. It is appropriate for the training professional to make recommendations in both areas because the goal is to help the business—not just to have a good training program.

Chris at Whitewater Outfitters is very cognizant of this human performance improvement role and takes it seriously. Check out Exercise 7-1.

Exercise 7-1. Whitewater Outfitters Case Study: Part 6

Table 7-1 provides the answers to Exercise 6-2. Compare your answers with these. If you missed a few, go back to part 5 of the case and work your way through the findings again.

Chris developed a list of training and nontraining recommendations for Emerson (the client) based on the data analysis. (Remember that Chris is a training professional within the HR department.) Compare your answers from Exercise 6-2 with Chris's. Here are his recommendations:

Training Recommendations:

Because the data analysis showed that the team leaders need to be able to conduct consistent, legal interviews and make consistent hiring decisions, they need training on the following skills:

- Design, develop, and deliver interview skills training for the team leaders.
  - o Learning objectives:
    - Prepare for an interview.
    - Analyze applications and resumes.
    - Develop focused, job-related interview questions.
    - Ask legal interview questions.
    - Conduct an interview.
    - Make a hiring decision.
  - o Content emphases:
    - legal interview questions
    - preparation for interviews
    - how to compare data to make an effective hiring decision.

Because the data analysis showed that the team leaders need to work collaboratively to have consistent interviews, the delivery method should be in an instructor-led classroom with team activities and role play.

- Delivery:
  - o Classroom.
  - o Pre-work (a reading assignment on effective interviewing that learners must read before coming to class).

- During the hiring push, convene two or three brown-bag sessions so learners can share what's working, not working, and their questions. They can take the new information back to the workplace immediately to continue improving their interviews.
- Learning activity parameters:
  - Provide opportunities for "bad" interviewing behaviors to be critiqued in a nonthreatening environment. (For example, critique the instructor role-playing a bad interview, or critique a video of a bad interview.)
  - Use multiple team-based learning activities. Gradually progress in activities until learners are comfortable working on some activities alone.
- Process standards:
  - active
  - experiential
  - high-energy
  - multiple opportunities to practice
  - iterative process: keep circling back to how one subject builds on the last subject.

Nontraining Recommendations:
- Conduct further research regarding the reasons behind the other two EEO complaints. There may be other factors operating here. If so, correcting the legal aspect of how interviews are conducted will not eliminate the EEO complaints.
- Consider evaluating staffing levels during midday because the data analysis showed added stress when production output requirements stayed the same, but lunch breaks meant there were less people on the floor.
- Offer data and assistance to the shipping department. It could use those data to determine any ways that production could offer assistance, or if there are other factors causing the glitches and negative customer feedback.
- Because there are problems with team leaders receiving so much negative feedback, give the production team leaders more specific reports on the causes of customer complaints; only offer constructive feedback on issues that are related to production.
- Because the majority of the customer complaints are due to shipping problems, coach the production team leaders to stop passing on critical feedback regarding customer complaints related to shipping rather than production.

- Consider developing a comparison of benefits programs between Whitewater Outfitters and Eddie Bean, the other sportswear company in town, to address the perceived issue of better benefits at Eddie Bean. If the comparison does not support the employee contention and perception, publicize it. If the comparison does indicate issues, consider conducting a benefits needs assessment survey to help decide whether the benefits program requires revision.

Now Chris must present the needs assessment results to Emerson. What suggestions would you offer Chris for planning and implementing the presentation?

Presentation goals:

Audience characteristics:

Media and handouts:

Presentation style:

Information to emphasize:

Things to watch out for:

Table 7-1. Data Analysis

Needs Assessment Stage	Data Analysis	Was Emerson Right (✓)?	Was Information New to Emerson (→)?	Training (T) or Nontraining (NT)?	Data Source
Stage 1: Business Needs	The upcoming hiring push will require the team leaders to have interviewing skills.	✓		T	Waddell (interview)
	Two of the four EEO complaints in the past fiscal year relate directly to team leaders having asked illegal interview questions.		↑	T	Extant data (HR)
	A glitch in the shipping process caused 85 percent of customer and retail store complaints in the past six months. Shipping is not part of the production process.		↑	NT	Extant data (complaint department)
	Turnover is higher than the industry average. There is a direct connection between the higher turnover and the following four factors:	✓			Waddell (interview)
	• Team leaders are making poor hiring decisions, resulting in turnover due to stress, burnout (in underqualified new hires), and boredom (in overqualified new hires).	✓		T	Waddell (interview) and extant data (exit interviews)
	• A common source of stress for all team members occurs during midday hours when fellow team members take lunch breaks and the same amount of work must be done with fewer people on the line.		↑	NT	Team leaders
	• Team members are stressed by the large amount of negative and critical feedback they receive from their team leaders regarding the perceived production problems (and team leaders are also getting the same negative and critical feedback).		↑	NT	Team
	• There is a common perception among employees that Eddie Bean's benefits are better than Whitewater Outfitter's.	✓		NT	Extant (exit interviews) and team leaders

Table 7-1. Data Analysis (continued)

Needs Assessment Stage	Data Analysis	Was Emerson Right (✓)?	Was Information New to Emerson (→)?	Training (T) or Nontraining (NT)?	Data Source
Stage 2: Performance Needs	Interview techniques are inconsistent among team leaders and vary from candidate to candidate. Team leaders need to conduct interviews that are consistent from team leader to team leader and from candidate to candidate.	✓		T	Interview experts, Waddell (interview), HR extant data, team leaders
	Little or no preparation is done for interviews, so team leaders will need to learn how to prepare for interviews.		→	T	Interview experts, Waddell (interview), HR extant data, team leaders
	Team leaders currently just ramble and chat during interviews, so they will need to learn how to structure interviews.		→	T	Interview experts, Waddell (interview), HR extant data, team leaders
	Interview questions are not well designed; they are obvious and leading. Team leaders need to ask well-designed interview questions so they can accurately assess candidates' potential fit for production jobs.		→	T	Interview experts, Waddell (interview), HR extant data, team leaders
	Team leaders are not familiar with and do not use legal, job-related interview questions. They need to start using them.	✓		T	Interview experts, Waddell (interview), HR extant data, team leaders
	Current hiring decisions result in mismatched hires at least 50 percent of the time. Team leaders need to use objective, consistent criteria to make well-matched hiring decisions.	✓		T	Interview experts, Waddell (interview), HR extant data, team leaders

Stage 3: Learning Needs	At the end of the training session, learners must be able to do the following: • Prepare for an interview. • Analyze applications and resumes. • Develop focused, job-related interview questions. • Ask legal interview questions. • Conduct an interview. • Make a hiring decision using objective criteria.	✓ ↑ ↑ ✓ ✓ ✓	T T T T T T	Interview experts
Stage 4: Learner Needs	The learners work mostly in teams with their own team or in a team of team leaders; they are not used to working alone.	↑	NT	Team leaders, prior instructors, prior course evaluation data
	The fast-paced, stressful environment allows little time to stay focused on one task.	↑	NT	
	The learners know that they need the training.	↑	NT	
	The learners are fearful of not doing well in training and being embarrassed.	↑	T/NT	
	The learners are not used to sitting in a classroom; they usually move around on the job.	↑	NT	

Well, you've reached your goal of producing training and nontraining recommendations based on your needs assessment study. Are you finished yet? Not quite! Now you must develop a method to present the data, analysis, and recommendations to your client. This task is examined in chapter 8.

8

Communicating With Your Client

 ## What's Inside This Chapter

This chapter presents communication techniques that can assist you in reaching your goal: the implementation of your recommendations. You'll learn:

- how to plan the presentation of needs assessment study results
- presentation tips.

Communicating With Your Client

The needs assessment study, data collection, and data analysis are now complete (Figure 8-1). Now it is time to present all this information to your client. Try to negotiate a feedback meeting when you present the needs assessment results to the client. You can also plan to augment the oral presentation with written materials.

Planning the Feedback Meeting and Presentation

The discussion that follows addresses the planning process for delivering the information to your client.

Define Your Presentation Goals

Presumably, the goals of your presentation are to persuade the client to agree to the training solution's design and delivery as recommended to improve the business and performance, and take ownership of any nontraining issues and recommendations. Do not forget these goals as you plan and deliver your presentation—each comment you make should draw the audience back to your goals.

 Basic Rule 24

The goal of the training needs assessment presentation is to generate decisions and actions on the part of the client to implement the training project.

Figure 8-1. The Training Needs Assessment Process With Step 6 Highlighted

Step 1. Conduct an External and Organization Scan

Step 2. Collect Data to Identify Business Needs

Capitalize on an opportunity
Resolve a problem
Support a strategy

Step 3. Collect Data to Identify Performance, Learning, and Learner Needs

Required performance
Learners' current performance
Required skills and knowledge
Learners' current skills and knowledge
Learner needs

Step 4. Analyze Data

Identify key data: gaps in performance,
skills, and knowledge
Identify recommendations

Step 5. Identify Potential Training Solution

Needed job aids and performance support materials
Types of training methods
Types of training delivery

Step 6. Deliver Data Analysis Feedback

Training recommendations: design and
delivery; ROI or ROE forecast
Nontraining recommendations: work
environment, rewards, consequences,
work processes

Transition Step: Begin Training Design

Know Your Audience

Do you know who will attend your presentation of data analysis and recommendations? Will it just be your client or will other key players be invited? Plan to address the interests of all concerned in the presentation. You should also plan to address the audience members' desired level of detail. How much information will they want? Are they interested in a brief presentation that cuts to the chase? Or will they be more interested in your methodologies and research?

Another factor to consider is who will make the presentation. Will the needs assessor make the presentation to the client and the stakeholders, or does the client need to be brought up to speed on the data and recommendations so he can make the presentation to the stakeholders, with you in the room to help answer questions? This will vary depending on the organization, client, and stakeholders, and your experience and role in the organization.

Separate Analysis From Recommendations

You need to make it clear that data analysis and recommendations are two separate phases of the project. This should be reflected in the outline of the presentation, in handouts and PowerPoint slides, in communications with the client prior to the meeting, and in your own preparation for the presentation. Make sure to follow through by addressing data analysis and recommendations separately during your presentation.

Tailor Your Presentation Media and Style

When choosing the media and presentation style for your recommendations and data analysis, consider the needs of you and your audience. This is where knowing the culture of the organization is helpful. Find out who needs to be in the room (or on the phone) for the presentation, and what their roles are within the organization. Who has the ultimate power of approving the project? Ask your client to help you put the presentation together, to make sure the style and content match what your key stakeholders are expecting.

Your choice of media should be based on its formality and what media your audience tends to expect. Generally speaking, the more self-contained your media are, the more formal they are. For example, PowerPoint is a more formal medium than a flipchart. If your organization tends to depend on one kind of media (for example, PowerPoint), plan to use it at least for transition titles from subject to subject to increase your audience's comfort level.

How formal (or informal) your presentation should be depends on your organization's culture and the client's style. Choose a setting that fits—a boardroom for a formal presentation or a conference table in an office for an informal presentation. Tailor your speaking and presentation style to the level of formality expected.

 Think About This

The level of formality of media also tends to imply the potential changeability of the content. When information is printed on a PowerPoint slide, it can send a message that the information is not up for revision. Flipcharts and handouts, on the other hand, signal less formality and rigidity. The audience will see content conveyed this way as more amenable to changes and revisions. This is why some needs assessors use multiple media in their presentations: a more formal, "rigid" method to present data analysis (because these are the facts that you discovered in your study) and a less formal, more easily modified medium for recommendations when the desired message to the audience is "Let's discuss these and revise as needed."

Handout Materials

Consider the level of detail that should go into the handouts and materials you are giving to the audience members. Will they simply want a brief outline with bullets to fill in with notes? Or are they looking for text-heavy, highly detailed information? Will they expect a two-page executive summary, accompanied by a detailed report? Do they want to see graphs and other visual presentations of the information?

Structure Your Time

Plan to use no more than half the allotted time to present your data analysis. The recommendation stage is the more important part of your presentation. You should allow sufficient time for your client to digest and discuss the analysis, and make the mental transition to recommendations (even perhaps identifying some of the recommendations in the discussion). You need to take into account the client's readiness factor before she will be open to discussing and hearing recommendations.

 Basic Rule 25

No one loves your methodology and data more than you do! Don't make the mistake of giving such a detailed explanation of them in your presentation that the recommendations portion is rushed or cut short.

Emphasize Information That the Client Can Influence

Highlight key data points that are within the client's power to do something about. You must acknowledge data that are unfortunate givens in the situation, but emphasizing them only makes the client feel powerless.

Plan Ahead

Give some thought to what you could cut from the presentation if it becomes necessary. This way, if the client is unexpectedly called away or walks in and says, "I know we scheduled an hour, but I'll have to leave in 30 minutes," you'll be able to adjust.

Making the Presentation

On some occasions and with some clients, the quality of your presentation can outweigh the quality of the actual needs assessment results. The presentation can be the convincing factor instead of the data. Don't make the mistake of thinking that your data can speak for themselves or that the answers are so glaringly obvious that you don't need to point them out. Remember, you have been intimately involved in and thinking about these data and the problem for weeks, but your client and the stakeholders probably haven't given it much thought. You need to be able to share a lot of information in a short time, and you need to be detailed enough that your client gets the importance of what you are sharing without the luxury of having lived and breathed the data for the past few weeks.

These are the factors that are most influential in a presentation:

- a level of detail that matches the audience's expectations and helps them understand the key issues involved
- your ability to answer questions that come up during the presentation
- organizing information to build evidence, so that the answers are logically presented to the audience
- your ability to link disparate points of information on the spot, making it obvious to the client that you truly understand the business issues.

The more you behave as if the information is so interesting that you are sure the trends and patterns are as obvious to the client as they are to you, the more convincing you will be to the client than if your behavior implies that you are trying to convince him that this is correct.

Basic Rule 26

If your client comes up with a recommendation before you present it, that's a good thing!

Also, think about your role in the presentation. During the data analysis portion of the presentation, your role should be that of presenter and observer; in the words of Sergeant Joe Friday, "Just the facts, ma'am." If the client asks what the data mean or what you think about the information, gently and firmly say that this will be addressed in the recommendations portion of the presentation. Later, during the recommendations, your role can change to that of an advocate for your recommendations.

An apt analogy for this presentation is a courtroom. Your client is the jury who will eventually make a judgment about your testimony. When you are presenting data, your role is that of an eyewitness: "This is what I saw and heard . . ." The data analysis is reported to the client with as little bias as possible. When you transition to recommendations, your role can change to that of an attorney who is actively trying to influence the jury's decisions.

Think About This

The parking lot technique that trainers use in training courses can be useful in your needs assessment presentation. When a client asks a question you would like to reserve for the recommendations portion of your presentation, note it on a flipchart or whiteboard and tell that client that this point will be parked there until it is addressed later.

Steps in the Presentation

1. Begin with a summary of what was done in the needs assessment study. Briefly share the methods you chose and why, as well as any significant developments that occurred during the data collection.

2. Present the data first. After you let the data sink in, ask the client what he thinks about the key data points. The client may arrive at some of the recommendations during the discussion of the data. Should this happen, the client's ownership of these recommendations will be assured. When presenting your data, be simple, concise, and

direct. Validate what the client has done right along the way, and position your study as augmenting and supplementing the client's efforts. Present new information that contradicts the client's initial problem or beliefs in a "Guess what I found?" mode, not a "You were wrong" mode. Don't try to fill dead air too quickly. Silence on the client's part can mean that she is thinking about the data. If the silence becomes uncomfortable, ask the client a question, but don't move on to the next data point yet. Expect some disagreement, rejection, or even disbelief of your information. Let your client digest and assimilate the information you have presented.

3. Make an obvious transition to recommendations. Turn the page, change the slide, take a break, or make a verbal transition: "Now that we have discussed the data analysis, I'd like to get into suggestions for what actions we can take based on this information."

4. Be flexible as the meeting goes on. If you have prepared well, the flexibility will already be built into your plan. You may need to move more quickly or more slowly through information, depending on the needs of your audience. You may also need to change media type. Have a formal PowerPoint presentation ready just in case the audience wants it. Or, be ready to move from PowerPoint slides to a flipchart or whiteboard if the audience wants to generate ideas on the spot.

5. Ask for what you want. As the presentation winds down, say, "Here is what I would recommend that we do." Then itemize what you will do to begin the design of the training program, and what you need from the client to address (or at least acknowledge) any nontraining issues. Together, develop an action plan to clearly outline the actions that you both will implement.

 Think About This

Using the passive voice is one way to make the client more comfortable. For example, you could say, "There are indications that the initial training program was incomplete," rather than, "There are indications that you didn't implement a complete training program." This way, you can avoid using accusatory language (the word *you* is a key offender), giving the client some intellectual distance from the data so they can be reflected upon, rather than defended against.

Next Steps

You also have to identify nontraining issues and recommend what should be done to address them. It is the client's prerogative to determine what actions will actually be taken, if any. A client may be unable or unwilling to address a nontraining issue. In that case, it is imperative that you get the client to acknowledge that the nontraining issue exists and that it will affect your performance and business goals. Do this before you proceed with the training design implementation. Once the project is finished and evaluated, you can point out whether or not the the nontraining issue had an effect on the desired performance and business goals.

Getting It Done

A presentation of needs assessment data and recommendations must be tailored to the client's style. Be cognizant of the client's business needs, allow opportunities for the client to develop recommendations that are then validated in the presentation, and acknowledge the importance of nontraining issues that are influencing the business and performance situation.

Exercise 8-1 concludes the Whitewater Outfitters case study.

Exercise 8-1. Whitewater Outfitters Case Study: Part 7

The table below lists some of the items Chris included in his presentation plan. Compare your answers from Exercise 7-1 with these. If you identified most of the same responses as Chris, congratulations! If you identified even more implications than Chris, you are clearly in sync with what makes a convincing presentation to a client.

Presentation Needs	Presentation Implications
Presentation goal	• Obtain Emerson's agreement to implement the training as recommended. • Obtain Emerson's acknowledgment that the nontraining issues will have an effect on the attainment of business outcomes.
Client Characteristics	**Presentation Implications**
Has a strong business need to support the hiring push	• Acknowledge the need up front in the presentation. • Continue to refer back to the business need in the presentation.

Client Characteristics	Presentation Implications
Communicated a simpler problem than the needs assessment revealed	• Validate the strong presenting need. • Acknowledge up front that you will deliver interview skills training and that it is an appropriate solution. • Position the needs assessment as a way to tailor the eventual training to the client's situation.
Has other business issues that could be related to the presenting problem	• Continue to refer to other business needs. • Set the expectation in the beginning that there may be some other answers for some of the business needs.
Has some assumptions about what training can do that are not accurate	• Provide a brief discussion of the role of training in addressing performance issues that are knowledge and skill related.
Was willing to give the benefit of the doubt to the needs assessor and allow access to data sources	• Express sincere appreciation for access to data sources and the client's organization. • Quantify the amount of time and organization resources it took to collect data and express the value of those data to the needs assessment outcomes.
Is sure about what needs to be done	• Continue to acknowledge that interview skills training will take place. • Emphasize that for the interview skills training to be a success, here is what else must be addressed (nontraining needs). • Be direct in asking for nontraining needs to be addressed.
Media and Handouts	**Presentation Implications**
	• Be results-oriented; the client wants the bottom line. • Offer facts and figures in easily understandable format: graphs, bullets, and so forth. • Continue to refer back to results measures that were presented as part of the problem.
Presentation style	**Presentation Implications**
	• Be informal, direct; don't beat around the bush. • Ask the client to speculate about what each key data point means as it is presented; help the client own recommendations later.
Information to emphasize	**Presentation Implications**
	• Keep coming back to the business and performance needs. • Continue to focus on the nontraining issues and recommendations.

Things to Watch Out For	Presentation Implications
Has a short timeframe in which to get ready for the hiring push	• Use language of urgency. • Be brief in each section of the presentation.
Has some incorrect assumptions about the causes for the presenting problem	• Validate all the correct assumptions. • Position new and contradictory information as interesting, not contradictory. • Use passive voice when appropriate.

Congratulations! You have now completed the training needs assessment study for Whitewater Outfitters. Now it's time for both needs assessor and client to get to work—Chris to design the training and Emerson to resolve the non-training issues.

This book began "near the end" because, like it or not, the training professional is often found at the end of the process—at step 5. Responding to a request for training by stepping back to step 2 to place the request in the context of the business needs is the necessary action to take when caught "in the middle." But, what would it be like if you could start at step 1? Chapter 9 presents that scenario.

9

The Ideal Organization Scan

 What's Inside This Chapter

This chapter goes beyond the real-world training needs assessment approach presented in this book. You'll learn:

- what the first two steps of training needs assessment are all about
- about sources of external and organization needs assessment information.

9

The Ideal Organization Scan

Chapter 2 opened with a scenario in which a department manager stops a training professional in the hall and formulates a training request. The training needs assessment approach in this book was based on that scenario because that's the way it happens in many organizations.

You will remember from the training needs assessment process (Figure 9-1) that this scenario depicts the training professional entering the process at step 5 (identify potential training initiative). This scenario requires the training professional to move back into step 2 (collect data to identify business needs) to place the potential training plan in the context of the business needs.

Were you wondering if the true beginning of the process would ever be addressed?

Now is that time. In a perfect world, training professionals would always be able to engage their clients in a proactive mode. They would consistently and constantly scan the organization (steps 1 and 2 in Figure 9-1) for indicators that business needs, performance needs, or both could be addressed by a training-related initiative. Trainers in this perfect world would then approach the potential client with that information and propose both training-related and nontraining-related initiatives. Only then would step 5 begin, which is where this book and your adventure in needs assessment started!

 Think About This

If the perfect-world scenario represents an ideal approach, then why don't training professionals use it more often? Because it is challenging enough to be effectively reactive, which is the approach presented in this book. Being effectively proactive and scanning the organization may seem far out of reach—will you ever have a solid week to conduct a thorough external and organizational scan? Not often. So, do it when you can. Even if you're usually in reactive mode, you will enhance your ability to discuss the business with the client and put the expressed training need in the business context.

Figure 9-1. The Training Needs Assessment Process With Steps 1 and 2 Highlighted

Step 1. Conduct an External and Organization Scan

Step 2. Collect Data to Identify Business Needs

Capitalize on an opportunity
Resolve a problem
Support a strategy

Step 3. Collect Data to Identify Performance, Learning, and Learner Needs

Required performance
Learners' current performance
Required skills and knowledge
Learners' current skills and knowledge
Learner needs

Step 4. Analyze Data

Identify key data: gaps in performance,
skills, and knowledge
Identify recommendations

Step 5. Identify Potential Training Solution

Needed job aids and performance support materials
Types of training methods
Types of training delivery

Step 6. Deliver Data Analysis Feedback

Training recommendations: design and
delivery; ROI or ROE forecast
Nontraining recommendations: work
environment, rewards, consequences,
work processes

Transition Step: Begin Training Design

Organization Scanning and Business Need Identification

Believe it or not, the most important guidelines for steps 1 and 2 of the needs assessment process are simple:

- Keep your eyes and ears open.
- Read every resource that you can get your hands on.
- Be a sponge; soak in information even if you don't know at the time how you will use it.

Training professionals are in a unique position in an organization and have access to many informal sources of information about the business and its environment. Employees tell them things that they might not tell others—even their managers. Trainers are also privy to information sharing in other departments when they conduct training. They serve on cross-functional committees and teams and, consequently, have extensive contact with people from other parts of the organization. They work on employee activities, such as annual picnics, and have contacts throughout the organization.

Remember that needs assessment and the resultant training solutions must focus on resolving a business problem, capitalizing on a business opportunity, or supporting a business strategy. As you implement the scanning process, keep focusing on these areas.

Basic Rule 27

Be a sponge. Soak up information from as many informal and formal sources as possible.

Sources of External and Organization Scan Data

Training professionals have access to multiple sources of formal information. Ideally, you should regularly interview your main potential clients. How often (monthly, quarterly, yearly) is up to you, but you need to keep your finger on the pulse of their business. Areas to focus on include the client's department mission, departmental strategies, operational goals, plans and objectives, and stated wants and needs.

In the course of your work, make an effort to keep up with external and internal sources:

- trade and industry journals and newsletters, publications such as *The Wall Street Journal* and *Businessweek*, and local and regional newspapers
- your organization's annual report
- competitors' annual reports

- stock market reports, if your organization is publicly traded
- your organization's mission statement
- your organization's strategic plans
- change implementation or reorganization plans regarding equipment, technology, work processes, automation, and business opportunities (such as new products, services, and markets)
- organizational climate indicators (such as labor and management relationships, grievances, turnover, absenteeism, suggestion box ideas, accidents, short-term sickness, observations of behavior, climate and attitude surveys, and the ever-present gossip)
- staffing issues and plans (such as long- and short-term workforce planning, succession planning, local and national demographics, industry indicators, job function indicators, and population growth)
- efficiency indicators (including productivity rates, labor costs, materials costs, product quality, equipment utilization, distribution costs, waste rates, downtime, late deliveries, repairs, operational reviews, and customer satisfaction)
- input of potential clients (such as department heads or managers)
- reward systems
- input from employees
- extant data from departments that regularly collect their own data (including HR, accounts receivable/payable, customer service, and quality).

 Think About This

Most departments that regularly collect extant data won't have a problem allowing you access because your request should be for *aggregate* data only. Training needs assessors don't focus on individual performance issues; those are for the managers of individual employees to deal with. For needs assessment, you need aggregate data that (you hope) will indicate trends and patterns for groups of employees.

Think of the external and organization scan as the investigative reporter approach. Reporters are exposed to many different sources of information, which means that they can put together seemingly disparate pieces of information and identify patterns that no one else can see. They are used to asking questions and digging deeper to get to the root cause of a problem. Then the

TV viewers or newspaper readers can say, "Of course! I see it now!" That's what this approach is about. All the information is out there—it just needs a fresh set of eyes looking at it in a different way. Table 9-1 offers some tips for using the investigative reporter approach.

Table 9-1. Tips for Using the Investigative Reporter Approach

Investigative Reporter Action	Ways to Do It
Get out into the organization on a regular basis.	Eat lunch with different people. Take your break in a different break room. Walk around the production floor and observe (with permission from the manager, of course!). Ask managers, for departments that you work with, to "ride along" or "sit along" with some of the employees in their department. The only way keeping your eyes and ears open will work is if you go to different places regularly.
Ask lots of "what" and "how" questions.	What do you mean by that? How would this look if it were different? What's happening that shouldn't be happening? What shouldn't be happening that is? How would you solve this if you could?
Think about things in different ways.	What is the root cause of this? How does this factor depend on others? What analogy would capture the way this process looks and feels? If this problem or challenge were facing _____, how would they handle it? (Pick an apt metaphor, for example a baseball team, church choir, or army platoon.)
Keep files of information in a way that makes it easy for you to rearrange them and see patterns.	Write notes on index cards or in files on your computer that can be copied and pasted. Maintain a file of clippings from internal and external sources.
Allow yourself thinking time when many patterns and big-picture concepts will occur to you.	Take a short walk at lunch. Use 30 minutes to look out the window. Hang a do-not-disturb sign on your office door for a few minutes each day.

Getting It Done

Now is your chance to think like a trainer in a perfect world. Use Exercise 9-1 to brainstorm ways that you can implement the investigative reporter approach to proactive organization scanning in your work as a training professional.

Exercise 9-1. Identify External and Internal Resources for Conducting Performance and Business Needs Scans

Take a look at the resources listed in the left column. Use the right column to jot down possible specific ideas about how you can access such resources within and outside your organization. Where relevant, note the name and position of the resources, or state the location of the source. The first row has a few examples to get you started, but there's space to add your own ideas.

Resource	Your Ideas
Trade and industry journals and newsletters	Executive office reception area Public library Public relations officer/corporate headquarters Sign-up for email alerts from industry sources
National, local, regional newspapers, and magazines	
Your organization's annual report	
Competitors' annual reports	
Stock market reports, if your organization is publicly traded	
Your organization's mission statement	
Your organization's strategic plans	
Change implementation or reorganization plans regarding equipment, technology, work processes, automation, and so forth	
Business opportunities (e.g., new products, service, markets)	
Organizational climate indicators (e.g., labor and management relationships, grievances, turnover, absenteeism, suggestion box ideas, accidents, short-term sickness, observations of behavior, climate and attitude surveys)	
Gossip and innuendo	
Staffing issues and plans (e.g., long- and short-term workforce planning, succession planning, local and national demographics, industry indicators, job function indicators, and population growth)	

Resource	Your Ideas
Efficiency indicators (e.g., productivity rates, labor costs, materials costs, product quality, equipment utilization, distribution costs, waste rates, downtime, late deliveries, repairs, operational reviews, customer satisfaction)	
Input of potential clients (e.g., department heads, managers)	
Reward systems	
Input from employees	
Extant data from departments that regularly collect their own data (e.g., HR, accounts receivable/payable, customer service, quality)	

You may have noticed that there is still one step remaining in the training needs assessment process—the transition from needs assessment into design. It is at this point that the needs assessor switches hats and either becomes the training designer or hands the design process over to an instructional designer. It is also the point where this book hands off the reader to other resources for the design process.

10

A Final Note

 What's Inside This Chapter

This chapter offers some food for thought about the role of training needs assessment in the organization. You'll learn:

- the most common errors that can occur in training needs assessment
- how strategic needs assessment is related to performance consulting or HPI.

10

A Final Note

Training needs assessment is the process of identifying how training can help your organization reach its business and performance goals. Often, its most valuable output (to the organization) is the identification of the nontraining factors that affect these goals. Other outputs include:

- the relationship between stated business and performance needs and the proposed training need
- the goals at each stage that will ultimately be evaluated in the training evaluation process
- training design indicators, such as learning objectives, learning activities, background, and content to help activities simulate the job environment
- metrics that will be used to measure learning success and business success during the training evaluation process.

Common Errors in Needs Assessment

It would not be right to leave you without a warning about the mistakes you can make in a training needs assessment. Here are the most common errors that occur:

- **Insufficient data collection or analysis:** You may choose not to conduct a thorough needs assessment, or perhaps the client pressures you to shorten these steps client. Make it clear at the outset what a proper needs assessment involves and get buy-in from your client.
- **Treating presenting problems only:** It's an error to assume that the client's only issues are the issues that she presented and then jump on the bandwagon to resolve those issues. Most of the time, the client's presenting problem is accurate, but it is not the only thing that is going on. Doing a needs assessment is the way to ferret out all training and nontraining issues.

- **Applying no tools or the wrong tools:** Always try to triangulate training and nontraining issues by using at least two different data collection methods. However, remember that it is also possible to use too many tools, leading to "analysis paralysis."
- **Trying a quick fix:** Take time to focus on the real problem rather than just treating the presenting problem symptoms.
- **Applying the wrong fix:** Avoid falling into the trap of just delivering what the client wants rather than what the client needs; sometimes it takes a while to see that "the training request in the hall" was the wrong fix.
- **Giving feedback in the wrong "language":** As a training professional, you're accustomed to using needs assessment or HRD jargon; make an effort to address clients and stakeholders in their own language (for example, costs, impact, and results).
- **Assuming one problem or one solution:** Very seldom is a performance or business issue the result of a single problem; there are nearly always multiple issues that require multiple solutions—perhaps a training initiative, perhaps not.
- **Failing to identify nontraining issues:** Whether it is because of pressure from the client, or your own choice, training to reduce a skill deficiency cannot change performance when there are other nontraining factors that also affect the performance.
- **Failing to educate clients regarding nontraining issues:** Allowing clients to continue to think that training is the only solution to performance problems does them a disservice because more often than not they won't be able to achieve their business and performance goals. If you don't address nontraining issues and fail to close the performance or learning gap, you're doing yourself a disservice and undermining your credibility.
- **Failing to consider the costs:** There are costs associated with everything an organization does. The costs may be calculated as time, resources, or even money. Make sure you bring up any costs associated with the needs assessment and the training and nontraining recommendations. This shows the client that you understand time and money are valuable and you are being respectful of any costs you are incurring or projecting. This also shows your clients that you speak their language.

The Problem With Needs Assessment

One major problem this book hasn't yet addressed is the amount of time and work that is needed to do a quality training needs assessment and address client expectations. A client may actually stop you in the hall on Monday and ask you to develop a training program for his department in four weeks. Why? Maybe he just found out that his entire sales team will be in town in four weeks and his leader has given him the responsibility of finding a solution for a major problem that needs to be resolved. Perhaps he had been trying to figure out how to solve the problem when he ran into you in the hall or on a conference call.

So what do you do in this situation? You know that you could conduct the training session in four weeks, but there is a strong likelihood that it won't solve the problem. You also know that you don't have enough time to do a complete needs assessment.

You first need to consider whether four weeks is long enough to design and deliver a training session. It could be, but it depends on the topic and scope of the project. Four weeks might be long enough to deliver some types of training programs if your training plan builds in additional time for training in the future. Armed with this information, you now need to determine what to do about the needs assessment. You know that you will have a better chance of meeting the organization's needs and helping them solve the problem if you perform a needs assessment.

There used to be a saying, "Fast, cheap, or good—pick two." The training industry was led by this mantra for many years. But today, clients want all three, especially when they hear about rapid development or rapid e-learning. So what is a training professional to do?

You need to say "yes, and" to the client like we mentioned in chapter 2. However, think about the access you will have to the data, the subject matter experts, and others who can give you information about the potential causes of the problem. Think about what you've learned in this book about conducting an effective needs assessment. What are three to four methods you could employ to incorporate a quick training needs assessment as part of your training design? You may be able to conduct both simultaneously to get a rough idea about what is causing the problem. Explain to your client that you will be able to meet some of the training needs in the time specified, but you should also do a needs assessment while designing the course. You will also need additional time and access to some of the subject matter experts after the course to evaluate whether it was able to address the root of the problem. Let your client know that you will likely want to do an additional needs assessment to determine whether or not further training and nontraining initiatives are necessary.

Another idea is to ask your client if you can use the time the sales team is in town to hold a focus group instead of a training session. In this scenario, you would develop and start your needs assessment plan before the sales team comes into town. Then during the sales team group session, you would ask them to share what's going on from their perspective, hear what they think is causing the problem, and ask what they think could be a solution. You could turn the training session time into a needs assessment focus group session where you gather information and data from the team that will be used later to provide some solutions to the problem. This method has the added benefit of building a culture of continuous improvement where everyone gets to help solve the problems. Use the data collected from this focus group session, along with the other data you gathered before the sales team came to town, to provide your client with training and nontraining recommendations.

What About Performance Consulting?

Two much-used terms in the HRD field these days are *performance consulting* and *human performance improvement*. While needs assessment seems very similar to performance consulting, they are not the same thing.

Here's why: Training needs assessment traditionally focuses solely on identifying the needs relevant to a planned training initiative. That means focusing only on data collection and analysis relevant to the content or the method of the training; that is, identifying and quantifying the skills to be learned in the training course, learning activities, and learner needs. Therefore the focus has always been on learning.

HPI is a more comprehensive approach that goes beyond just training. Performance consulting is a cyclical, systematic, and systemic process that looks at all areas of the organization and even the organization's influence on society. The ATD Human Performance Improvement Model, shown in Figure 10-1, walks performance consultants through the full model, starting with business analysis to performance and key performance analysis to evaluation and results. This is an iterative process. You can see how the arrows move in and out of each step and how they are interconnected. As you start to implement each part of this model, you begin to move from training consultant to performance consultant.

Critical components of HPI or performance consulting include (Piskurich 2002):
- focusing on business and organization goals
- using a systematic approach based on desired results
- focusing on accomplishments and performance
- linking performance analysis to the job
- analyzing performance gaps
- identifying training initiatives that will close the performance gaps

- planning and implementing solutions
- evaluating results
- focusing on business and organization goals.

Figure 10-1. ATD Human Performance Improvement Model

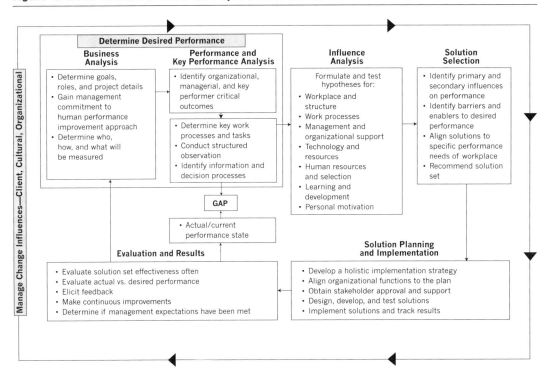

In HPI, three types of initiatives can be applied to address performance gaps:

- **Motivational initiative:** Inserting into the organization various incentives, rewards, and outcomes for desired performance that will influence job performers to choose to perform to standards.
- **Structure and process initiatives:** Making changes in organizational structure, reporting relationships, work processes, feedback, and procedures to influence job performance and results.
- **Knowledge and skill initiatives (training):** Imparting knowledge and skills to job performers in a way that will improve performance and results.

Sound familiar? It should—it is the approach presented in this book but with a few twists. You might call it the HPI training needs assessment approach. The training needs assessment presented here is focused on identifying required job performance, ensuring that the desired job performance is supported by training, and checking to see that all other factors affecting job performance are also addressed. In responding to a training request, the training professional still begins with the business needs and context, focuses on the performance that is required to meet the business needs within that context, and then refocuses on the learning that must take place to support that required performance. The result of this approach is that the needs assessment study leads to training recommendations (how training solutions should be implemented), and nontraining initiatives (motivational, structural, and process), all of which will support job performance and organization goals.

HPI begins by identifying desired organizational results and performance, and identifies all types of potential solutions. The training needs assessment discussed in this book begins with desired training results, steps back to place the desired training results in the organizational and performance context, and identifies training initiatives and other solutions that will help, and not hinder, the performance.

 Noted

Are there occasions when an HPI approach will reveal that only motivational or structural process initiatives are necessary and no training solutions are needed? Yes, but so will this training needs assessment approach. You could conceivably respond to a client's training request by conducting a training needs assessment, only to find that the desired performance is being affected solely by nontraining issues. Just as with HPI, you would identify these issues and make recommendations to the client.

Perhaps the biggest difference between traditional training needs assessment and the HPI training needs assessment approach is also the simplest. Traditional training needs assessment focuses solely on ensuring that the ultimate training design will support employee performance by gathering information to support the training design, identify and capture skills and knowledge, and ensure that the design replicates the learners' jobs as closely as possible. The HPI training needs assessment approach goes beyond the training design—it results in recommendations regarding nontraining issues that are affecting the achievement of the desired organization and employee performance goals.

Remember that the most important question to ask yourself is this: *If the ultimate training program is perfect, what else is going on in the organization that will result in the business needs not being met?*

 Basic Rule 28

Call yourself an HPI consultant, a performance consultant, a training professional, or a needs assessor, as you like. Know that what you do has a complete focus on business, performance, learning, and learners.

Back in chapter 2 we mentioned that your ultimate goal as a training professional is to move from training order taker to training professional and finally to performance consultant. When you employ the systematic and systemic process of human performance improvement, you help your organization by focusing on the right things, not just the training things. But it takes a lot of courage to move from training order taker to performance consultant. Why? Because when you try to help the organization by taking in the big picture and thinking about the organization as a whole, you step out of your comfort zone of just thinking about training needs (remember, when all you have is a hammer, everything looks like a nail) and you step out of the mold that clients and business partners have put you in.

When you start to think strategically, you start to act strategically. Your needs assessment will be viewed as a strategic advantage and a benefit to the organization. Other departments will start to notice the benefit and positive effects your training department is having on the departments you work with. You will be able to influence and mentor other training professionals to help them move from training order takers to performance consultants. As a result, the organization will prosper.

Conclusion

Find ways to make this approach your own. Suggested reading and references are provided in the back of the book to assist you in developing your skills. Remember to use the process to build credibility for your approach and to continue to drive to the role of performance consultant. Have confidence in your abilities to expand the perception and role of the training professional in your organization. Remember, when a training program adds value the training function will be valued for its impact and results. A training program adds much more value to the organization when it is focused on performance improvement and organization results, and when all factors that affect performance and training effectiveness are considered.

References

Block, P. 2000. *Flawless Consulting*, 2nd edition. San Francisco: Jossey-Bass/Pfeiffer.

Fuller, J. 1999. "Understanding Human Performance Improvement." In *Performance Interventions: Selecting, Implementing, and Evaluating the Results*, edited by B. Sugrue and J. Fuller. Alexandria, VA: ATD Press.

Kirkpatrick, J.D., and W.K. Kirkpatrick. 2011. "Creating ROE: The End Is the Beginning." *T+D* 65(11): 60-64. www.td.org/Publications/Magazines/TD/TD-Archive/2011/11/Creating-ROE-the-End-Is-the-Beginning.

Mager, R.F. 1997a. *Analyzing Performance Problems*, 3rd edition. Atlanta: Center for Effective Performance.

Mager, R.F. 1997b. *Making Instruction Work*, 2nd edition. Atlanta: Center for Effective Performance.

McCain, D. 2016. *Evaluation Basics*, 2nd edition. Alexandria, VA: ATD Press.

Phillips, J.J., and P.P. Phillips. 2016. *Real World Training Evaluation*. Alexandria, VA: ATD Press.

Piskurich, G. 2002. *HPI Essentials*. Alexandria, VA: ATD Press.

Rossett, A. 2009. *First Things Fast: A Handbook for Performance Analysis*. San Francisco: Wiley.

Zemke, R., and T. Kramlinger. 1982. *Figuring Things Out: A Trainer's Guide to Needs and Task Analysis*. Reading, MA: Addison-Wesley.

Additional Resources

To support you in your continuous learning, the following list of sources used and additional reference material is provided. The listing of reference material is divided into categories to help you find a source you may need. This is not an exhaustive list by any means; rather, it is a beginning point for you.

Needs Assessment

Bartram, S., B. Gigson, and B. Gibson. 2000. *The Training Needs Analysis Toolkit*. Amherst, MA: HRD Press.

Gilbert, T.F. 2007. *Human Competence: Engineering Worthy Performance (Tribute Edition)*. San Francisco: Pfieffer.

Gupta, K. 1999. *A Practical Guide to Needs Assessment*. San Francisco: Jossey-Bass.

Harless, J. 1970. *An Ounce of Analysis Is Worth a Pound of Objectives*. Newnan, GA: Guild V Publications.

Harless, J. 1973. "An Analysis of Front-End Analysis." *Improving Human Performance: A Research Quarterly* 4: 229-244.

Harless, J. 1976. "Speaking From Experience." *Training and Development Journal* 30(3): 10-11.

McClendon, M.J. 2003. *Statistical Analysis in the Social Sciences*. New York: Wadsworth Publishing Company.

Phillips, J., and E.F. Holton III. 1995. *In Action: Conducting Needs Assessment*. Alexandria, VA: ASTD Press.

Phillips, L. 1994. *The Continuing Education Guide: The CEU and Other Professional Development Criteria*, 3rd ed. Dubuque, IA: Kendall-Hunt Publishing Company.

Pike, B. 1994. *Managing the Front-End of Training*. Minneapolis: Lakewood Books.

Ripley, D.E. 1997. "Joe Harless, Ed.D.: An Ounce of Analysis." In *Performance Improvement Pathfinders: Models for Organizational Learning*, edited by P.J. Dean and D.E. Ripley, 92-107. Washington, DC: International Society for Performance Improvement.

Rossett, A. 1987. *Training Needs Assessment*. New York: Educational Technology Publishers.

Rossett, A. 2009. *First Things Fast: A Handbook for Performance Analysis*. San Francisco: Wiley.

Sparhawk, S., and M. Schickling. 1994. "Strategic Needs Analysis." *Infoline*. Alexandria, VA: ASTD Press.

Spencer, L.M., and S.M. Spencer. 1993. *Competence at Work*. New York: John Wiley & Sons.

Sprinthall, R.C. 2002. *Basic Statistical Analysis*. Boston: Allyn & Bacon.

Swanson, R. 1996. *Analysis for Improving Performance*. San Francisco: Berrett-Koehler Publishers.

Adult Learning

Brown, P.C., H.L. Roediger, and M.A. McDaniel. 2014. *Make It Stick: The Science of Successful Learning*. Cambridge, MA: The Belknap Press of Harvard University Press.

Carey, B. 2015. *How We Learn: The Surprising Truth About When, Where, and Why It Happens*. New York: Random House.

Dirksen, J. 2015. *Design for How People Learn*, 2nd ed. San Francisco: New Riders.

Knowles, M. 1990. *The Adult Learner: A Neglected Species*, 4th ed. Houston: Gulf Publishing.

Knowles, M., E.F. Holton, and R.A. Swanson. 1998. *The Adult Learner: The Definitive Classic in Adult Education and Human Resource Development*, 5th ed. Houston: Gulf Publishing.

Merriam, S.B., ed. 2001. *New Directions for Adult and Continuing Education*. San Francisco: Jossey-Bass.

Merriam, S.B., and R.S. Cafarella. 1998. *Learning in Adulthood: A Comprehensive Guide*. San Francisco: Jossey-Bass.

Vella, J. 2002. *Learning to Listen, Learning to Teach: The Power of Dialogue in Educating Adults*. San Francisco: Jossey-Bass.

Facilitation Skills and Facilitator Competencies

Bentley, T. 1994. *Facilitation: Providing Opportunities for Learning*. New York: McGraw-Hill.

Eitington, J.E. 2001. *The Winning Trainer: Winning Ways to Involve People in Learning*, 4th ed. Boston: Butterworth-Heinemann.

Hunter, D., A. Bailey, and B. Taylor. 1995. *The Art of Facilitation*. Tucson, AZ: Fisher Books.

Justice, T., and D.W. Jamieson. 1999. *The Facilitator's Fieldbook*. New York: AMACOM.

Kearney, L. 1995. *The Facilitator's Toolkit*. Amherst, MA: HRD Press.

Kinlaw, D. 1996. *The ATD Trainers Sourcebook: Facilitation Skills*. New York: McGraw-Hill.

Leatherman, D. 1990. *The Training Trilogy: Facilitation Skills*. Amherst, MA: HRD Press.

Rumsey, T.A. 1996. *Not Just Games: Strategic Uses of Experiential Learning to Drive Business Results*. Dubuque, IA: Kendall-Hunt.

Shapiro, L.T. 1995. *Training Effectiveness Handbook*. New York: McGraw-Hill.

Wheeling, S.A. 1990. *Facilitating Training Groups*. New York: Praeger.

Instructional Design and Development

Anderson, L.W., D.R. Krathwohl, P.W. Airasian, K.A. Cruikshank, R.E. Mayer, P.R. Pintrich, J. Raths, and M.C. Wittrock. 2001. *A Taxonomy for Learning, Teaching, and Assessing: A Revision of Bloom's Taxonomy of Educational Objectives*. New York: Pearson, Allyn & Bacon.

Anglin, G. 1991. *Instructional Technology: Past, Present and Future*. Englewood, CO: Libraries Unlimited.

Barca, M., and K. Cobb. 1994. *Beginnings & Endings: Creative Warm-Ups & Closure Activities*. Amherst, MA: HRD Press.

Broad, M., and J. Newstrom. 1992. *Transfer of Training*. Reading, MA: Addison-Wesley.

Carliner, S. 2015. *Training Design Basics*, 2nd ed. Alexandria, VA: ATD Press.

Charney, C., and K. Conway. 1998. *The Trainer's Tool Kit*. New York: AMACOM.

Clark, R.C. 2014. *Evidence-Based Training Methods*, 2nd ed. Alexandria, VA: ATD Press.

Clark, R.C., and R.E. Mayer. 2016. *E-Learning and the Science of Instruction: Proven Guidelines for Consumers and Designers of Multimedia Learning*, 4th ed. San Francisco: Wiley.

Engelhart, M.D., E.J. Furst, W.H. Hill, and D.R. Krathwohl. 1956. *Taxonomy of Educational Objectives, Handbook I: The Cognitive Domain*. Edited by B.S. Bloom. New York: David McKay Co.

Gagne, R. 1985. *The Conditions of Learning*, 4th ed. New York: Holt, Rinehart & Winston.

Keller, J.M. 2010. *Motivational Design for Learning and Performance: The ARCS Model Approach*. New York: Springer.

Merrill, M.D. 2009. "First Principles of Instruction." In *Instructional Design Theories and Models: Building a Common Knowledge Base*, vol. 3, edited by C.M. Reigeluth and A. Carr. New York: Routledge Publishers.

Nadler, L. 1989. *Designing Training Programs: The Critical Events Model*. New York: Addison-Wesley.

Phillips, J., and M. Broad. 1997. *In Action: Transferring Learning to the Workplace*. Alexandria, VA: ASTD Press.

Silberman, M., and K. Lawson. 1995. *101 Ways to Make Training Active*. San Diego: Pfeiffer.

Stolovitch, H.D., and E.J. Keeps. 2011. *Telling Ain't Training: Updated, Expanded, Enhanced*, 2nd ed. Alexandria, VA: ASTD Press.

Thiagarajan, S., and T. Tagliati. 2011. *Jolts! Activities to Wake Up and Engage Your Participants*. San Francisco: Wiley.

Thiagarajan, S., and T. Tagliati. 2012. *More Jolts! 50 Activities to Wake Up and Engage Your Participants*. San Francisco: Wiley.

Measurement and Evaluation

Brinkerhoff, R.O. 1987. *Achieving Results From Training*. San Francisco: Jossey-Bass.

Brinkerhoff, R.O. 2006. *Telling Training's Story: Evaluation Made Simple, Credible, and Effective*. San Francisco: Berrett-Koehler.

Dixon, N. 1990. *Evaluation: A Tool for Improving Quality*. San Diego: University Associates.

Kirkpatrick, D.L., and J.D. Kirkpatrick. 2006. *Evaluating Training Programs: The Four Levels*, 3rd ed. San Francisco: Berrett-Koehler.

Kirkpatrick, J.D., and W.K. Kirkpatrick. 2016. *Kirkpatrick's Four Levels of Training Evaluation*. Alexandria, VA: ATD Press.

Phillips, J. 1996. *Accountability in Human Resource Management*. Houston: Gulf Publishing.

Phillips, J.J., and P.P. Phillips. 2015. *Real World Training Evaluation*. Alexandria, VA: ATD Press.

Swanson, R., and E. Holton. 1999. *Results? How to Assess Performance, Learning, and Perceptions in Organizations*. San Francisco: Berrett-Koehler.

Performance Consulting

ASTD Press. 2001. "A Guide to Performance." *Infoline*. Alexandria, VA: ASTD Press.

Langdon, D.G., K.S. Whiteside, and M.M. McKenna, eds. 1999. *Intervention Resource Guide: 50 Performance Improvement Tools*. San Diego: Pfeiffer.

Robinson, D.G., and J.C. Robinson. 1989. *Training for Impact: How to Link Training to Business Needs and Measure the Results*. San Francisco: Jossey-Bass.

Rothwell, W.J. 2013. *Performance Consulting: Applying Performance Improvement in Human Resource Development*. San Diego: Pfeiffer.

Rummler, G. 2004. *Serious Performance Consulting According to Rummler*. Silver Spring, MD: ISPI; Alexandria, VA: ASTD Press.

Silberman, M., ed. 2001. *The Consultant's Tool Kit*. New York: McGraw-Hill.

Willmore, J. 2016. *Performance Basics*, 2nd ed. Alexandria, VA: ATD Press.

Presentation Skills

Becker, D., and P.B. Becker. 1994. *Powerful Presentation Skills*. Chicago: Irwin Professional Publishing.

Burn, B.E. 1996. *Flip Chart Power: Secrets of the Masters*. San Diego: Pfeiffer.

Jolles, R.L. 2000. *How to Run Seminars and Workshops: Presentation Skills for Consultants, Trainers, and Teachers*. New York: John Wiley & Sons.

Peoples, D.A. 1997. *Presentations Plus: David Peoples' Proven Techniques*, rev. ed. New York: John Wiley & Sons.

Pike, R., and D. Arch. 1997. *Dealing With Difficult Participants: 127 Practical Strategies for Minimizing Resistance and Maximizing Results in Your Presentations*. San Francisco: Jossey-Bass.

Rosania, R. 2003. *Presentation Basics*. Alexandria, VA: ASTD Press.

Silberman, M., and K. Clark. 1999. *101 Ways to Make Meetings Active: Surefire Ideas to Engage Your Group*. San Diego: Pfeiffer.

Stettner, M. 2002. *Mastering Business Presentations*. McLean, VA: The National Institute of Business Management.

Zelazny, G. 1999. *Say It With Presentations: How to Design and Deliver Successful Business Presentations*. New York: McGraw-Hill Trade.

Strategic HRD

Chalofsky, N.E., and C. Reinhart. 1988. *Effective Human Resource Development*. San Francisco: Jossey-Bass.

Gilley, J., and A. Maycunich. 1998. *Strategically Integrated HRD: Partnering to Maximize Organizational Performance*. Reading, MA: Addison-Wesley.

Hudson, W. 1993. *Intellectual Capital: How to Build It, Enhance It, Use It*. New York: John Wiley & Sons.

Pershing, J.A., ed. 2006. *Handbook of Human Performance Technology*, 3rd ed. San Diego: Pfeiffer.

Sevenson, R., and M. Rinderer. 1992. *The Training and Development Strategic Plan Workbook*. Englewood Cliffs, NJ: Prentice Hall.

Miller, L., and M. Homan Blanchard. 2013. *Coaching in Organizations: Best Coaching Practices From the Ken Blanchard Companies*. Self-published.

Murphy, M. 2011. *Hard Goals: The Secret to Getting From Where You Are to Where You Want to Be*. New York: McGraw-Hill.

Walton, J. 1999. *Strategic Human Resource Development*. London Guidhall University: Financial Times/Prentice Hall.

About the Authors

Beth McGoldrick is an instructional designer for RiverSource Insurance, part of Ameriprise Financial, where she has won awards for training projects she designed and developed. She has more than 18 years of experience in training and development in the insurance industry and academia, including skills in analyzing, designing, developing, and measuring training.

Beth has written articles and book chapters on various training topics, including needs analysis, instructional design for mobile learning, and evaluation. She mentors other instructional designers throughout the country. She has a master of science in organizational performance and workplace learning from Boise State University.

Beth lives in Minneapolis, Minnesota, with her husband, John, son, and Shetland sheepdog. Beth may be reached at BethMcGoldrick.ISD@gmail.com.

Deborah D. Tobey has 20 years of experience in the organization development and HRD field. She is currently the director of talent management for the Tennessee State Department of Safety and Homeland Security, and an adjunct senior lecturer at Vanderbilt University. Her areas of specialization include training needs assessment, design, facilitation, and evaluation; consulting skills and systems development; group processes and team building; competency modeling; and leadership development.

In her private consulting practice, Deborah's clients have included state and local governments, universities, nonprofit organizations, and Fortune 500 organizations in the manufacturing, finance, import, healthcare, and service sectors. She served in a full-time teaching role at Vanderbilt University, as well as in numerous appointments in adjunct roles, most notably at George Washington University and Vanderbilt University. She is the author or co-author of several ATD publications.

Deborah has a bachelor's degree in English and a master's degree in student personnel administration and counseling, both from Virginia Tech. Her doctorate in HRD is from Vanderbilt University. She lives in Nashville, Tennessee, and may be reached at ddtobey@gmail.com.

HOW TO PURCHASE ATD PRESS PUBLICATIONS

ATD Press publications are available worldwide in print and electronic format.

To place an order, please visit our online store: www.td.org/books.

Our publications are also available at select online and brick-and-mortar retailers.

Outside the United States, English-language ATD Press titles may be purchased through the following distributors:

United Kingdom, Continental Europe, the Middle East, North Africa, Central Asia, Australia, New Zealand, and Latin America
Eurospan Group
Phone: 44.1767.604.972
Fax: 44.1767.601.640
Email: eurospan@turpin-distribution.com
Website: www.eurospanbookstore.com

Asia
Cengage Learning Asia Pte. Ltd.
Phone: (65)6410-1200
Email: asia.info@cengage.com
Website: www.cengageasia.com

Nigeria
Paradise Bookshops
Phone: 08033075133
Email: paradisebookshops@gmail.com
Website: www.paradisebookshops.com

South Africa
Knowledge Resources
Phone: +27 (11) 706.6009
Fax: +27 (11) 706.1127
Email: sharon@knowres.co.za
Web: www.kr.co.za

For all other territories, customers may place their orders at the ATD online store: **www.td.org/books**.